LEARNING

ENVIRONMENTS

FOR CREATIVITY

a toolkit for k-12 school design

for architects, administrators, teachers, parents and community

MACKENZIE SIMS

DEDICATION

To the students whose voices, spoken and unspoken, inspired this project.

To the outstanding teachers in the trenches who dedicate their lives to future generations.

To the child in all of us, who yearn to play and imagine, explore, and make mud pies.

To Clark Hagen and Madilyn Werner, may your education and school inspire and support you to thrive.

This project is for you.

Architectural Design Strategies

 Campus + Building Security

 Open Space

 Landscaping - Green Space

 Daylighting

 Indoor/Outdoor Environments

 Spaces for Exercise

 Varied Sizes of Spaces

 Informal Learning Spaces

 Flexibility

 Air Quality - Natural + Mechanical

 Thermal Comfort

 Technology: Teaching Tools

 Technology: Building Systems

 Furniture, Fixture + Equipment

 Electrical Lighting

 Acoustics

 Materiality

GLOSSARY OF SYMBOLS

Nine Principles of Learning Environment for Creativity

 Safety

 Healthy Building

 Direct Access to Natural Environments

 Physical Activity + Room to Run

 Visual Connection to Nature

 Teaching + Learning

 Flexibility + Ownership

 Spaces + Atmospheres

 Playfulness

ACKNOWLEDGEMENTS

This book would not have been possible without a tremendous amount of help and involvement from countless people. First and foremost, thank you to my advisors Vuslat Demircay, Leigh Ann Pfeiffer, and Kurt Hunker for providing guidance, a wealth of resources, enthusiasm and endless support. Their diversity in perspectives and backgrounds helped manifest this multi-disciplined study come to fruition.

Thanks to principal at Vista Elementary School, Charlene Smith and Executive Director of Facilities and Operations for Vista Unified School District, Brock Smith for their guided tour of Vista Elementary and the preceding discussion.

To my dear friend Marysa Loyle for helping me edit this book, but even more so for being an inspirational teacher. Your dedication to your students and loving reminders of what it really looks like to be a teacher in American schools helped shaped this book more than you know.

A special thanks to my father, Brian Sims, for allowing me to use him as a sounding board and always being there for creative brainstorming sessions.

To all the teachers, students, designers, architects, superintendents, who have inspired and fueled this project, thank you.

DESIGN PRINCIPLE DEVELOPMENT

BACKGROUND

The design of an elementary school must be carefully aimed to enhance the engagement, and ultimately the creative process of children. Creativity can be broadly understood as the connection of knowledge in unique ways (Dietrich, A, 2004), (Corpley, A, 1995), (Piffer, 2012). This is vital in a child's education. Being able to make connections and communicate ideas not only prepares students to be strong, active citizens, but also increases the interest in learning, and discovering new information. However, these processes are difficult to measure precisely and are misunderstood in developing brains of children, compared to matured, adult brains (Craft, A., 2001).

Designing the ideal learning environment for young children requires close examination of many factors. This study will focus on attainable data that directs the design of a school to provide better learning environments and encourage children's imagination, creativity and ultimately their personal learning outcomes regardless of the student's background. These factors include: the current/future education pedagogies, neurological and psychological child development specifically pertaining to creative processes, and the physical built environment.

The figure on the follow page illustrates the research framework for this Toolkit.

P

PREFACE

THE METHOD

This study examines the impact of learning environments on student creativity and well-being. The research includes an investigation of educational philosophies of the 21st Century, cognitive psychology of childhood development, learning and creativity, the current and historical conditions of school architecture. Based on this multidisciplinary evidence principles of creative learning and architectural strategies were developed to support children's health, well-being and creativity. In additional to reviewing the research across disciplines, this project involved industry engagement through site visits to schools under construction and completed, a focus group discussing the realities of implementing evidence based design into the practice of architecture, and a symposium bridging community engagement, physical learning environments and students.

SAFETY

Create a space that is safe for children to explore, but not so safe they don't learn how to manage danger.

HEALTHY BUILDING

Design a school that does not hinder the health of the users (air quality, natural ventilation, thermal comfort, etc)

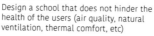

DIRECT ACCESS TO NATURAL ENVIRONMENTS

Allow exploration and physical interaction with natural outdoor environments and fresh air.

HEALTH + WELLBEING

VISUAL CONNECTION TO NATURE

Provide visual connection from interior spaces to the surrounding natural environment, either to landscaping or the sky or both.

PHYSICAL ACTIVITY + ROOM TO RUN

Indoor and outdoor spaces to run free. Allow students to explore independently and have fun.

FREEDOM TO EXPLORE

TEACHING + LEARNING

Peak student interest/engagement through different teaching methods and exercises.

FLEXIBILITY + OWNERSHIP

Use customization and flexibility to empower students to feel ownership of a space. Let them create their own interest within a space.

INTEREST + CURIOSITY

SPACES + ATMOSPHERES

Diversity of spaces. Peak curiosity as students move throughout and around the school.

PLAYFULLNESS

Allow students to explore ideas. Create a space where students are comfortable speaking up and experimenting.

DESIGN PRINCIPLE DEVELOPMENT

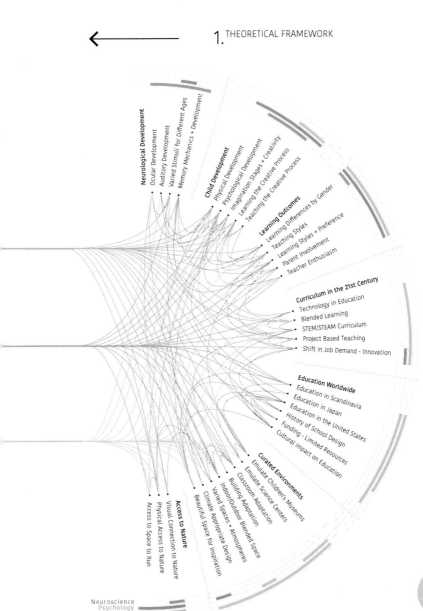

Neurological Development
- Ocular Development
- Auditory Development
- Varied Stimuli for Different Ages
- Memory Mechanics + Development

Child Development
- Physical Development
- Psychological Development
- Imagination Stages + Creativity
- Learning the Creative Process
- Teaching the Creative Process

Learning Outcomes
- Learning Differences by Gender
- Learning Styles
- Teaching Styles + Preference
- Learning Styles + Preference
- Parent Involvement
- Teacher Enthusiasm

Curriculum in the 21st Century
- Technology in Education
- Blended Learning
- STEM/STEAM Curriculum
- Project Based Teaching
- Shift in Job Demand - Innovation

Education Worldwide
- Education in Scandinavia
- Education in Japan
- Education in the United States
- History of School Design
- Funding - Limited Resources
- Cultural Impact on Education

Curated Environments
- Emulate Children's Museums
- Emulate Science Centers
- Classroom Adaptation
- Building Adaptation
- Indoor/Outdoor Blended Space
- Varied Spaces + Atmospheres
- Climate Appropriate Design
- Beautiful Space for Inspiration

Access to Nature
- Visual Connection to Nature
- Physical Access to Nature
- Access to Space to Run

Neuroscience
Psychology
Education
Architecture

INTRODUCTION

School design is undergoing a major shift. Curriculum, teaching methodologies and policies are being reevaluated. The education system is no longer about producing young adults to work in factories or specialized, single-task oriented, production line jobs. This shift in education has been underway for decades. Curriculum and teaching methodologies are changing, but the physical environments in which learning happens, have, for the most part, not been updated to meet these changing needs. This leaves teachers and students confined to inflexible, outdated learning environments, forced to 'make do' with highly restrictive, sub par environments.

In an era where the rate of change continues to increase and the future job demands remain uncertain, a close examination of education tactics and learning environments is necessary. We must evaluate not only the way students are taught and the way they learn, but also the **space in which they learn**. Many of the existing learning environments today are detrimental, both physically and mentally, to students and teachers. These spaces, built for a production-line mentality, are often in a state of degradation, overdue for modernization. They have poor air quality, limited

"We are getting ready to run a bond in April and one of our platforms is that our elementary school has outdated classrooms. I was hoping you could help point me in the direction of some up-to-date research about the impacts facilities have on learning."

- Selah School Dist. Superintendant

access to daylight and nature. Population fluctuations leave the buildings over-crowded or under-utilized. Conditions like these impede learning, interest and creativity for those inhabiting the space.

By focusing on student's physical and cognitive needs for enriched, diverse environments, that **children want to be in**, schools can encouraging exploration and curiosity, and ultimately nurture student and teacher creativity.

WHY NOW?

January 29th, 2018 at a public hearing in Olympia, Washington regarding a Senate Bill to increasing Capitol Funding to Public k-12 schools three high schools students testified to the Senate Ways & Means Committee (Senate Ways & Means Committee, 2018). The first student, a Junior at Sequim High School said,

> "I will be walking across the stage next year with my diploma never having taken a science class in a real lab setting. Students from other districts who can consistently pass bonds have the opportunity to take classes in updated and state of the art facilities. How are my peers and I from Sequim getting equipped with the skills necessary to be competitive with these students in the 21st century work place? It's not fair. It's not right. And it's time to get started and to not shy away from these issues any longer"

The second student, a Junior at Port Angeles High School, says his school, built in 1955, has three big issues in a school that is essentially "falling apart": water, heating, and electrical. He goes on to describe the degradation of the facilities, the two remaining water fountains that still work, the uncomfortable fluctuation of temperatures at both extremes; overheated and insufficient heating in classrooms across campus. He even mentions the roof falling in at one point. He says "schools are supposed to be welcoming; like a second home to students and building conditions are directly linked to a student's engagement and willingness to learn."

The last student describes the stark differences between the two schools her parents work at. Her mother works at a school that was built in 1927 and hasn't seen a significant renovation. The conditions are poor, with inadequate lighting, undersized electrical systems that require resetting the fuses when they blow from being overused. The plumbing is 80 years old, the HVAC doesn't run properly, and for recess the students walk several blocks to a near by park because there isn't a playground on campus.

Contrasting this is the school that her father teaches at. His school was built in 1992 and upgraded in 2004 and the only notable problem is "the mid-aged roof, which is to be expected." Other than this, the facility ranks in the 90th percentile. The difference between these two schools is due to the districts they are in. The students' father's school is in a district which passes bonds regularly and has high property values, and thus higher taxes compared to the district where her mother teaches.

" How are my peers and I from Sequim getting equipped with the skills necessary to be competitive with these students in the 21st century work place?"

- High School Junior

These testimonials are not novel, they are a snap shot of many of the issues students today are facing from kindergarten through high school. These inadequate facilities are directly impacting students mental and physical health, their willingness to learn, and their capacity to absorb information and think creatively.

INTENT OF TOOLKIT

The intent of this Toolkit is to provide a concise set of evidence based principles and strategies for designing environments that support student engagement and nurture learning and creativity. The information is intended for a wide audience. Students, teachers, parents, school administration, district facility staff, politicians, architects, designers and the community at large who are invested in improving the state of schools in the United States can learn from this book. Significant change requires a movement that includes everyone involved. This Toolkit provides a base knowledge, backed by research, to ignite a conversation and enact change moving forward. The information outlined in this book aims to educate stakeholders and help the designer create better spaces for children, their health and well-being, and their ability to learn and be creative.

"Knowledge isn't poured into children, like water into a vase. Instead, children are constantly creating, revising, and testing their own theories about the world as they play with their toys and friends."

-Mitchel Resnick

HOW TO USE

Designing environments for creativity is not simply about picking parts from a catalog. It is about ensuring a holistic intent centered around the learners and their needs. Whether you are a parent, a politician, a teacher or an architect there is information in the Toolkit which will benefit you. Section 2: Advocate + Educate outlines a holistic approach to learning environments for creativity, both from an educational perspective and physical environment. This section is the ground work for the conversation that is taking place in communities, school districts, and state governments. It is the foundation for understanding how the education system and subsequent built environment impacts student's learning, well-being and creativity.

If you are involved in the design of schools, from renovations, to transformations, to new construction, section 3 and 4, Project Integration and Design Strategies, respectively, dive deeper into architectural specifics that influence student well-being and creativity. This section outlines how to implement design strategies into a project's design time-line, who to involve in the conversation, and how often.

CASE STUDY: MONTE VISTA ELEMENTARY SCHOOL

The Monte Vista Transformation project follows design strategies outlined in this book, following the research in neurological development, child psychology, education demands of the 21st Century, and school architecture. This approach allows schools to modify, or transform an existing facility or create a new campus depending on their needs and budgets. Monte Vista Elementary School (MVES) represents a typical condition – an existing, suburban neighborhood school.

This project serves as an example of how to implement the ideas outlined in the Toolkit for a typical mid-century school. Depending on your school's condition, and budget available for renovation, transformation or a new school, the examples in this book are intended to spark ideas for your given circumstances.

Designing the ideal learning environment for young children is not prescriptive. It requires close examination of multi-layered factors. This promotes better learning environments that encourage children's imagination, creativity and ultimately their personal learning outcomes. Working within an existing framework, this proposal transforms MVES into a school that inspires students, teachers and parents to get involved and to manifest creativity integral with education.

PROJECT INFORMATION

Location:	Vista, California
Student Body:	~550, projected 600 by 2025
Age Group:	Kindergarten - 5th Grade
Original Construction:	1964
Site Area:	10.8 Acres
Existing Building Size:	54,887 ft^2
Landscape + Fields:	424,561 ft^2
Original Classrooms:	14
Portable Classrooms:	Original: 5, Additional: 18
Total Classrooms:	37

The school is operating out of a facility that no longer meets the needs of the district goals, the curriculum, or the students. The typical California finger plan has seen several additions and relocatables added over the years – now representing nearly 60% of classrooms on campus. The original permanent buildings are of good structural standing, an appropriate scale for small children but lack in adequate daylight and visual and physical access to the natural surroundings. The teachers attempt to utilize outdoor learning as much as possible, however the restrictions of the portable building configuration and designed outdoor space is limiting. The majority of teachers have reassessed and removed the outdated rows of desks in their classrooms, replacing them with various seating arrangements that the students vote on and are assigned a new seat each week.

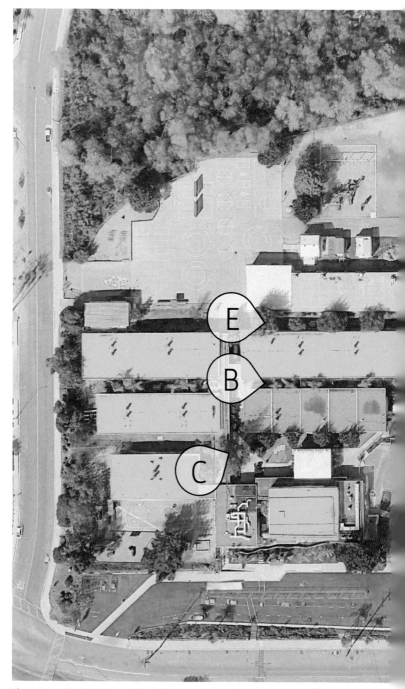

Figure 1.1 Existing site diagram with photographs indicated (see figure 1.2)

Original permanent structures

EXISTING CONDITION OBSERVATIONS

Progressive pedagogy in place: most teachers have removed typical desks from the classroom. Every classroom we visited there were mixed learning environments from 2 person desks to large round tables to lounge chairs to beanbags. One teacher said she has the kids rate what kind of seat they would like for the week and are assigned a designated seat for the week based on their ratings.

College-Bound Theme: Each teacher hangs their college flag outside their classroom and the students talk about college and have healthy rivalries between different colleges. One class sang us the ASU fight song!

Outdoor Learning: The space between the original buildings (non-portable from 1963) provides accessible break out areas but needs more shade. The spaces between the original buildings and the semi-permanent portables (added in the 80's) was under-utilized due to a railing barrier built around the portable/modular buildings. Teachers and principals desire more outdoor learning.

Gardens: There are a few gardens on site as well as a garden classroom. The gardens are part of the curriculum and students grow crops from seedlings, calculate crop outcomes and sell the produce. They use this as an exercise in gardening as well as business and entrepreneurship.

Portables: All portables have minimal windows and no plumbing. Portable classrooms account for over 50% of the classrooms on campus.

Play Space: The site includes a lot of hard-scape with negligible shade. Covered play shed is required augmented by landscaped areas.

Figure 1.2 Existing site photographs (see figure 1.1)

Advocate | Educate

Figure 2.1 Thriving Plant
Environment

2

ADVOCATE + EDUCATE

The quality of school facilities is reliant on more than school construction. While this Toolkit focuses on the design process and design measures that influence creativity of the students, the ground work begins before the client engages the architect for a design. Part of the role of the architect is to educate the community of the importance of school design. This ranges from providing the school board current information of impactful of spaces on children's learning and well-being to testifying in front of the state legislative representatives to increase capital funding.

The work fundamentally begins with understanding creativity and its critical importance, establishing that creativity is not a set of hard-and-fast rules that must be followed, but instead something that can be nurtured and thrive in the correct environment. Much like how a plant needs specific environmental settings (figure 2.1) in order to grow, a child needs a specific environment to learn.

> "The [creative] process is like that of a farmer or gardener taking care of plants by creating an environment in which plants will flourish "
>
> –Mitchel Resnick

The information in this book provides a foundation of evidence based design and the science of creativity. Implementing change within the education system in the United States requires an understanding of how the physical environment impacts children and teachers, but also requires advocacy at all levels of the system and evaluation of systems other than architecture.

EDUCATION REFORM

The current education system is experiencing a paradigm shift in curriculum, teaching and learning methodologies and facilities design (Lippman, 2010) (OCED, 2011) (Cannon Design, VS Furniture, & Bruce Mau Design, 2010). In order to design appropriately for the future generations, designers must step back from the design and first understand what children need in order to learn.

"We're running education systems where mistakes are the worst thing you can make. We're educating people out of their creative capacities"

–Sir Ken Robinson

Historical pedagogies, where the teacher holds the knowledge and stands in front of a class of 30 students in rows of desks are beginning to dissolve. Teachers are becoming facilitators of information, pulling from sources far greater than ever before (PK Yonge DRS., 2012) (Cannon Design, VS Furniture, & Bruce Mau Design, 2010). Evidence suggests that students learn more effectively through various types of exercises and teaching methodologies. Project-based learning is being implemented into curricula and proving to be a far more effective way of teaching young minds.

Some programs already focus on different pedagogies including Charter and Montessori schools and other specialized schools, both public and private.

CREATIVITY LENS

The English Dictionary (Dictionary, 2018), defines school as: "an institution designed to provide learning spaces and learning environments for the teaching of students." But a school, and the education system should do more. A school should provide a place to learn and foster creativity, and keep children excited about learning. Creative thinking is at the core of this.

Creativity, creative thinking, and creative learning are used at a lens to understand if a child is making connections beyond simple informative learning. Learning by definition is the "acquisition of knowledge or skills through experience, study, or by being taught" (Dictionary, 2018). Creativity takes what is learned and makes new connections, or applies the knowledge in new ways.

Just as a farmer or gardener creates a condition in which their plants will thrive, a learning environment must be constructed to support and nurture creative thinking. This requires the space to be flexible, safe and welcoming, engaging, and appropriately stimulating to all senses.

This is important to understand when design spaces that foster such cognitive functions. This, in conjunction with spaces in which children are comfortable, healthy and interested can help provide a nurturing environment that promotes exploration of ideas and excitement to learn.

THE NEED FOR CREATIVITY

The future job market is unpredictable. Jobs are changing as routine tasks become automated. Historically many jobs have been based on production line tasks and as a result education has been focused around the same, training people to follow the rules, perform a task and not deviate. As the economy changes the need to adapt increases. The driving force of the economy and society is now information instead of industry. People are expected to adapt with this technology, and deal with uncertainties that accompanies rapidly changing means of communication. "Roughly two-thirds of today's grade school students will end up doing work that hasn't been invented yet." (Resnick, M., and Robinson, K., 2017)

Creativity is now imperative beyond the workplace. The Information Age is impacting the way people communicate, the dynamic of relationships and the oscillating needs of their communities. With the rapid rate of change and the demands of the modern world, creativity and the ability to adapt are required to thrive.

"You can learn more about a person in an hour of play than a year of conversation"

- Plato

As a result of the changing times, the uncertainty of future conditions and the change in work force demands, children need to learn from an early age to be adaptive and creative in many aspects of their lives.

DEFINITION OF CREATIVITY

In the article "Cognitive Neuroscience of Creativity," author Arne Dietrich explains that creativity happens when existing pieces of knowledge, information, or experiences, are connected in a unique way. This is primarily achieved the prefrontal cortex of the brain. While the prefrontal cortex is not responsible for receiving or interpreting incoming sensorial information, it is responsible for working memory and integration of temporal information. This is the process of integrating highly processed information to enable higher cognitive functions, including creativity. The temporal information includes all sensorial data and long term memory. "It is this superimposing of already highly complex mental constructs that dramatically increases cognitive flexibility" (Dietrich, A, 2004).

Creativity is defined in adults as a process of connecting two or more "bits" of information in an innovative way. This is understood, but difficult to measure in the brain. Creativity doesn't happen in one part of the brain and cannot be accurately measured. In children, these concepts are even more difficult to understand. What can be determined, through interaction and observation of children, is if they are making connections novel and useful considering their limited base knowledge.

Creativity is more easily understood in adults than children. Adult brains are fully developed and thus connections are better understood and more consistently measured. Understanding creativity in a child's brain is difficult for several reasons. The first is their brains are still developing which makes it difficult to translate what we know about adult creativity to a brain that is not yet mature.

Additionally, measuring creativity is difficult and often determined based on the ideas or products an individual creates (Piffer, 2012). This testing technique doesn't work on children because they are still learning how to be creative.

There are myriad theories and methodologies for teaching different forms of creativity including problem solving exercises. Historically, it was understood that the process of creativity involved evoking surprise, or a novel idea (connecting two things in a new way) with the validation of establishing relevance of the idea. Evolving beyond this notion, teachable steps can be outlined as: preparation, incubation, inspiration, verification, communication and validation (Corpley, A, 1995).

Preparation involves the acquisition of knowledge, through experiences, and formal and informal education.

Incubation is the translation/transition of newly acquired information from working memory into long term memory—procedural, or episodic.

Inspiration is the surprise moment, when two or more seemingly unrelated pieces of information are configured in a new way. This "ah ha" moment releases the same endorphins as laughing, triggering a pleasure reward.

Verification is the evaluation of the new solution to see if it makes sense and is applicable to the problem at hand.

Communication and validation require the explanation of your idea to peers or teachers.

Each step of the process has different actions or opportunities associated with it. Figure 2.2 shows actions with each step that teachers can help facilitate.

Throughout this entire process (preparation thru validation), students are learning how to communicate, how to think, and how to apply the knowledge they have gained through education and experiences. This sounds procedural, implying that if you follow this every time you want to "be creative". This also implies that everyone has the same potential to be creative. Both statements have not been proven to be true. Additionally, there is often resistance to encouraging creativity in the classroom because it is misconceived as encouraging "unruly, disobedient, careless, imprecise, or just plain naughty behavior." (Corpley, A. 1995). However, a teacher can promote specific behaviors, such as looking at something in a new way, experimenting with different arrangements of information, or collaboration with other students. Even with teachers encouraging creativity in the classroom, research shows that children only "display creativity when they want to and when they feel able to." (Corpley, A. 1995). The question arises: how can we get children interested, comfortable and engaged with their education? How does the built environment impact this?

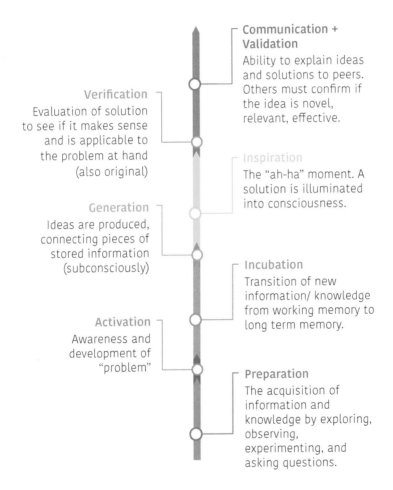

Communication + Validation
Ability to explain ideas and solutions to peers. Others must confirm if the idea is novel, relevant, effective.

Verification
Evaluation of solution to see if it makes sense and is applicable to the problem at hand (also original)

Inspiration
The "ah-ha" moment. A solution is illuminated into consciousness.

Generation
Ideas are produced, connecting pieces of stored information (subconsciously)

Incubation
Transition of new information/ knowledge from working memory to long term memory.

Activation
Awareness and development of "problem"

Preparation
The acquisition of information and knowledge by exploring, observing, experimenting, and asking questions.

Figure 2.2 Creativity Process, diagram by author based on (Corpley, A, 1995)

EDUCATION PEDAGOGY

Advocate | Educate

From a very young age, children are taught subjects in a disconnected, information based way. The current educational curriculum can be described as disconnected subjects taught in hour long segments; an hour of math, and hour of social studies, an hour of biology, etc. Subjects are not necessarily integrated. This way of teaching is rooted in the time this curriculum was developed when jobs were centered around production. With the production line mentality, schools were focused on students learning specific information through memorization. The means of assessing if a student had learned the material was through work sheet format tests, verifying that the student remembered what they were told during class. This way of standardized testing measures the ability of a student to memorize dates in history, follow directions and perform arithmetic. In this setting, the worst possible outcome is a wrong answer (Resnick, M., & Robinson, K., 2017).

"We don't stop playing because we grow old; we grow old because we stop playing"

– George Bernard Shaw

This is slowly starting to change with the use of project base learning rather than instructional learning. Emerging curriculum is more integrated, learning the subject matter required to complete a given project. Throughout the course of a project a student may need to learn some science, some history, some mathematics, and a lot of problem solving. This is a different way of teaching and learning than recent historical approaches. This approach helps children integrate and apply information to real life situations. Shifting the emphasis to problem solving also requires more creative thinking, team work, and communication.

Project based teaching has historically been a part of kindergarten but only recently is being translated into higher grade curriculum. In "Lifelong Kindergarten" cultivating creativity though projects, passion, peers, and play" by Mitchel Resnick (2017) outlines why approaches used in kindergarten need to be taught throughout primary school and beyond. Resnick defines two types of student: "A" students and "X" students. "A" students are what most people think of as exemplary students, achieving 'A' grades in their classes and high test scores on standardized tests. This type of student was ideal when jobs were task oriented, relating to the production line mentality the current education system in the United States is built on. However, "A" students, according to Resnick, "lacked creative, innovative spirit needed to be successful in today's society." On the other hand, there are "X" Students, who are willing to take risks, try new things, and define new problems, rather than solve those laid out in the textbook. In the United States, and most other developed countries, the emphasis is placed on teaching students to follow instructions and rules, becoming "A" students rather than on helping students develop ideas, goals and strategies, becoming "X" students.

In order to encourage students to take risks, learn from their mistakes, follow their intuition and learn to think creatively - all behaviors of "X" students - Resnick has developed the "four P's of Creative Learning."

- Projects: Learning centered around a single project, learning the information needed to problem solve and complete the project.

- Passion: Developing projects the students are passionate about will increase motivation and effort.

- Peers: Creativity is a social process, collaborating, sharing and building off of one another's ideas. Ensuring an atmosphere in which students can share their ideas.

- Play: Exploring ideas through experimentation, risk taking, and a playful spirit. These new interactions will uncover new types of projects and new directions.

This is essentially outlining a new way of structuring curriculum. Instead of focusing on information delivery and regurgitation via worksheets, this new approach focuses on idea exploration. This means that curriculum, lectures and homework all change. This type of project based learning is often used in Kindergarten and is lost in higher grade levels. Retaining this process in higher grade levels will encourage creative thinking and help the students build the habit of problem solving.

LEARNING THROUGH MAKING

The shift towards more project based learning is also supported by the Maker Movement. This builds on the increasingly advocated approach of "learning by doing," arguing that children learn best when they are actively involved in hand's-on activities. The Maker Movement takes this a step further by saying simply doing isn't enough, instead children should be making something to really learn. As the patron saint of this Movement, Seymour Papert says "Knowledge isn't poured into children, like water into a case. Instead children are constantly creating, revising, and testing their own theories about the work as they play with their toys and friends" (Resnick, M.,Robinson, K., 2017).

THE SCIENCE OF CREATIVITY

Creativity is a higher cognitive function, only possible after other human needs are met. Encouraging creativity in the learning process deepens the level of student engagement and motivation for executive function performance. Executive functions are cognitive processes the support the regulation of behavior, decision making and setting and achieving goals. Focusing on these processes in an holistic manor promote connections in different parts of the brain beyond the prefrontal cortex, in other words, more creative thought (Rasti, I., 2018). Creativity is considered one of the characteristics of self-actualization of Maslow's hierarchy of needs and the highest level of Bloom's Taxonomy of Educational Learning.

The brain processes information through the Reticular Activation System (RAS), which filters nearly all incoming data, giving priority to novel stimuli. Novel stimuli that enter the brain release the neurotransmitter hormone dopamine, increasing the sense of pleasure, alertness, memory and motivation by presenting information in a novel way. Novelty is triggered through environmental shifts, movement, humor, change of voice or multi-sensory methods (Rasti, I., 2018). In a school setting, much of this is done through the interaction between the teacher and the student, and between peers, however the built environment also has an impact. If the surrounding environment has insufficient or excessive background sensory stimuli, then new information may be difficult to process.

"A creative act is an instance of learning... [and that] a comprehensive learning theory must take into account both insight and creative activity"

- J.P. Guilford 1950

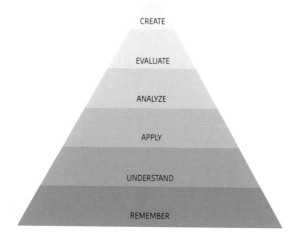

Figure 2.3 Bloom's Taxonomy
of Educational Learning based
on (McLeod, S., 2017)

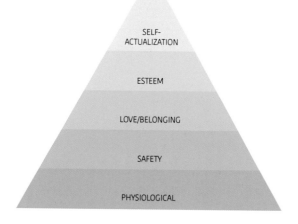

Figure 2.4 Maslow's Hierarchy
of Needs based on (Rasti, I.,
2018)

ENRICHED ENVIRONMENTS AND NEUROPLASTICITY

Learning is reliant on neuroplasticity; the ability of neurons to change and reorganize based on experiences and the environment. At the Academy of Neuroscience for Architecture (ANFA) Conference in 2016, Margaret Tarampi addressed how enriched environments impact neuroplasticity. This concept is important for creative thinking because it is at the foundation of absorbing and processing new information. Tarampi explains that neuroplasticity is depended on an individuals genetics, the environment they are in and the actions they take within that environment. Studies show that enriched environments; meaning enriched for visual, motor, cognitive, somatosensory that the environment can support, increase neuroplasticity and learning. By increasing the neuroplasticity in the brain, it increases the "size of the cortex, the length of neurons, the number of synapses, and the level of neurotransmitters and growth hormones," all of which are involved in the process of creative thinking (ANFA Conference 2016). The built environment can either foster or detrimentally harm this neural plasticity.

Healthy social engagement also plays a roll in learning, and neuroplasticity and the physical environment promotes different types of social interactions.

COGNITIVE PSYCHOLOGY AND ENVIRONMENT

Creativity takes time. Students must be allowed to explore ideas and create iterations in order to develop a creative idea, regardless of their cognitive styles. Creativity does not always occur immediately or spontaneously. Establishing an environment with mutual respect and acceptance between students and between students and teachers will allow for students to be comfortable sharing, developing and learning from their ideas. This also encourages team work as well as independent exploration (Fasko, D, 2001).

Two types of cognitive styles that relate to insight: assimilators and explorers. Assimilators give priority to upholding cognitive economy, meaning they prefer to perform tasks in which they have a high level of experience in. Explorers on the other than tend to seek new solutions and new ways of approaching problem solving. Explorers prefer to perform tasks with a high level of novelty compared to assimilator Each type of student requires a different type of motivation to find a balance between expertise and exploration.

The necessary environment to promote creativity includes both the physical surrounding environment, the perceived environment, and the mental environment of the student. The creative climate is important to stimulate creative thinking, this includes the physical environment as well as the teacher attitude, student and peer attitudes, comfort, etc. An important component of creativity is failure, or mistakes. Rather than a mistake being the worst possible outcome, as it is currently enforced through standardized testing and curriculum, create and environment where students learn from, and build on their failures. By helping students recognize why something failed, they will learn to correct as they go and feel comfortable enough to share ideas even if they may be less than ideal.

Creative thinking is above and beyond procedural or analytical learning. Traditionally, the mainstream education system in the United States teaches analytical learning, which is tested via State issued Standardized Testing. This measures how well a student can perform arithmetic, comprehend reading, and

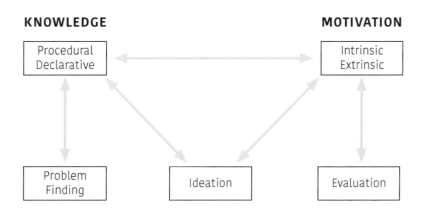

KNOWLEDGE

MOTIVATION

Procedural
Declarative

Intrinsic
Extrinsic

Problem
Finding

Ideation

Evaluation

Figure 2.5 Knowledge, motivation and problem solving, based on (Fasko, 2001)

various other prescriptive tasks. While this knowledge is important, learning should not end there. Creative learning connects disciples, applies knowledge to real like problems, and sparks innovation. Creativity is reliant on the base knowledge traditionally taught in school, but is also dependant on an individuals motivations, enthusiasm and willingness to experiment and problem solve in unique ways. Creative thought is increasingly accessible when the student is motivated and has a choice in the direction of pursuit. Fasko (2001) explains that students motivation is dependant on the meaningfulness of the task to the students, and this happens when they choose the tasks.

Figure 2.5 shows the two-tier model of creative thinking. The primary tier is founded with a set of skills or knowledge. Tier two develops problem identification, problem definition, ideation and evaluation. Ideation is the fluency of idea generation originality and flexibility. This requires a certain level of comfort with failure risk and iterative development. Evaluation includes assessment of the quality and relevance of the generated ideas (Fasko, 2001).

Student engagement, excitement and motivation are complicated and dynamic. The physical environment is only one factor. At minimum the physical environment should not be detrimental to the occupants. If this is the case, the built space becomes a blank canvas, a backdrop upon which the remaining factors build on. At best, the physical space enhances the perception of the environment, excites those within the space and promotes exploration and activity. However, if the teacher fails, or the student is physically or mentally uncomfortable, creativity and learning is hindered.

CREATIVE LEARNING SPIRAL

The creative learning spiral is an approach to teaching that allows students to learn throughout the course of a project. This approach is often used in Kindergarten or in Montessori Schools, with the new curriculums implementing this in higher grade levels.

The creativity spiral can be used at any stage of learning but it most effective if used early and often, forming cognitive habits of making connections, and confidence in exploring ideas. For example, consider children building a castle out of wooden blocks inspired by a story told to them by their teacher. The kindergarten students began to build on one another's ideas while narrating the developing scene, following the cycle of imagine, create, play, share, and imagine again (figure 2.6).

- Imagine: The students imagine the castle described in the fairy-tale the teacher shares. They start imagining the family that lives there, and what they do.

- Create: The children build a tower element of the castle out of wooden blocks.

- Play: As they build, they are constantly tinkering and experimenting, trying to build a taller tower without the tower falling over. Some students are building, some students are thinking about a story about the family, remembering the story they heard before and thinking about what else they may do.

- Share: These stories are told amongst the group, some children taking the lead on building, others on the verbal story telling, additional ideas are formulated from this collaboration; the students are excited.

- Reflect: When the tower collapses, the teacher encourages them to contemplate why it fell and figure out what they could do to make a more stable tower. The teacher shows them images of skyscrapers, and the children realize they are usually wider at the base, rebuilding accordingly.

- Imagine: Based on these experiences, the children develop new ideas and continue asking questions; can there be a village surrounding the castle, how about a puppet show in the village.

This process continues and creates opportunities to learn along the way in many subjects. While this example is fundamental, the same idea can be implemented for different ages, different topics and with more complexity as needed (Resnick, M.,Robinson, K., 2017.) This approach shifts the focus from the delivery of information to the exploration of ideas and problem solving.

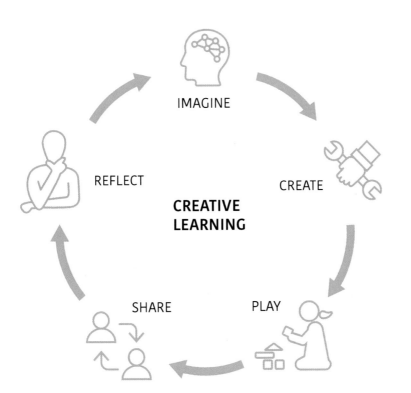

IMAGINE

REFLECT

CREATE

**CREATIVE
LEARNING**

SHARE

PLAY

Figure 2.6 Creative Learning Spiral.
Diagram by author, based on (Resnick,
M., Robinson, K., 2017)

CREATIVITY MISCONCEPTIONS

The value of creativity is misconstrued due to misconceptions in the educational system. These misconceptions include how creativity is expressed, who possesses it, how it is taught, and the defining moment of creative thought.

MISCONCEPTION: CREATIVITY IS ABOUT ARTISTIC EXPRESSION

One assumption that is made about creativity is that it is primarily about artistic expression, and those without artistic talent do not possess creativity. While artists are creative people, creativity is not specific to any discipline. Anyone can be creative, including scientists, doctors, entrepreneurs, social workers, mathematicians, politicians, etc. (Resnick, M., Robinson, K., 2017.)

MISCONCEPTION: ONLY A SMALL SEGMENT OF THE POPULATION IS CREATIVE

Creativity is also culturally misunderstood, in the United States, as only being accessible to a small number of people, such as Nobel Prize winners, or famous artists. Creativity is a skill and can be cultivated by anyone and expressed countless ways. Resnick (2017) describes two types of creativity. Big-C Creativity is considered the monumental discoveries, like the invention of the paper clip, or the light bulb. On the other hand there is little-c creativity, which is a new connection of information that helps serve a purpose; an idea for something useful in your everyday life.

MISCONCEPTION: CREATIVITY COMES IN A FLASH OF INSIGHT

Creativity has historically been described as an "ah ha!" Moment, but this is only one small component of the creative process. As Constantin Brancusi, a modern art pioneer said, "creativity is not being hit by a lightning bolt from god." (Resnick, M.,Robinson, K., 2017.) Instead it is a process that requires exploration, experimentation and systematic investigation.

MISCONCEPTION: YOU CANNOT TEACH CREATIVITY

This misconception is actually true to an extent. If teaching creativity is attempted by declaring a set of rules in a specific order, then creativity cannot be taught. There is no declarative time line for achieving creative thought. Instead creativity requires nurturing, encouragement and support. The process is like that of a farmer or gardener taking care of plants by creating an environment in which the plants will flourish.

Some people suggest the optimal way to support creativity in children is to merely get out of their way and let the child's natural curiosity lead the way. Children are naturally curious but the environment needs to be set up in a manner to encourage exploration of those ideas and further develop their ability to think creatively. (Resnick, M.,Robinson, K., 2017.)

THE BUILT ENVIRONMENT IMPACT

Most of the research to date involving creating a healthy school environment focuses on creating a space that does not impede the learning abilities of the occupants. This is done through evaluation and finessing of sensorial input. Environmental factors include air quality, thermal comfort, quality of natural and electric light, acoustic conditions, and visual stimuli, etc. But this isn't the entire picture. Other important factors include the students' emotional wellbeing (at home and at school) and how they feel when they go to school, or sit in a classroom. The perception of the space is vital to student success.

A study in England (Barrett, Davies, Zhang, & Barrett, 2015) looking at a holistic approach to environmental impacts on student learning indicates that while all of these categories are important, some make a larger impact on improving student progress than others. The study evaluated existing schools throughout England using three categories of consideration: Naturalness, Individualization and Stimulation (see figure 2.7).

- **Naturalness** includes natural and electric light, noise level, temperature and control of thermal comfort, air quality (based on CO_2 levels present) and adjust-ability of air exchange, and links to nature visually and directly.

- **Individualization** focuses on ownership and flexibility of the space. How a space can be customized, rearranged, and the level of connectivity to the rest of the school.

- **Stimulation** concentrates on sensorial information within the learning space, ranging from complexity of the room and layout to the color choice to the amount of decoration or excess noise (measured in naturalness but influences stimulation).

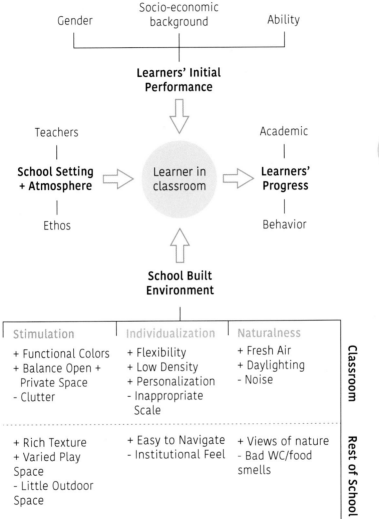

Stimulation
+ Functional Colors
+ Balance Open +
  Private Space
- Clutter

Individualization
+ Flexibility
+ Low Density
+ Personalization
- Inappropriate
  Scale

Naturalness
+ Fresh Air
+ Daylighting
- Noise

+ Rich Texture
+ Varied Play
  Space
- Little Outdoor
  Space

+ Easy to Navigate
- Institutional Feel

+ Views of nature
- Bad WC/food
  smells

Classroom

Rest of School

Advocate + Educate

Figure 2.7 Environmental Impact on Student Progress, based on (Barrett, Davies, Zhang, & Barrett, 2015)

After evaluating each of the classrooms, the study found that naturalness was the largest contributor to student academic progress. Maximizing indirect daylight warranted the greatest improvement. However, direct sunlight during parts of the day were found to create glare and discomfort. In addition to the natural light, the quality of electrical lighting makes a significant impact. Classrooms with high quality and good distribution of light saw the most student progress. Another significant contributor was decreasing the CO_2 levels in the room, this can be done via natural ventilation or improved mechanical air exchange. With increased natural ventilation and improved mechanical systems the perceived thermal comfort and control greatly improved. That study showed that academic performance improved in classrooms with more control over temperature fluctuations.

Individualization and stimulation results varied with age groups. In younger children, greater diversity of learning environments is desirable. Irregularly shaped classrooms help create nooks and study areas for varied physical environments that allow for students with different learning styles to thrive. These spaces can be customized and provides students with a strong sense of ownership. However, this level of individualization also increase visual stimuli. This showed to be positive with younger students. Older students performed better in more visually simplified classrooms with some individualization, but with a simply shaped room and less visual stimuli than in the classrooms for younger children. Additionally, it was found that exhibiting student work throughout the school, not just in the classrooms, helped encourage ownership and boost self-esteem of the students at all ages.

Research in visual stimulation shows that some use of color, on an accent wall can help create a positive mood in the classroom, but too much, or too vibrant color will tip the stimuli scale to excessive and distracting. Both under stimulating and overstimulating rooms performed poorly in this study.

While these environmental factors are vital for a healthy building and productive workspace, it lacks an understanding of what children actually desire in their educational settings. In the process of examining educational spaces to find the ideal environment for children to learn, we must see what the users prefer and what they are excited about. This was exactly what a study in Finland looked at (Kangas, 2010). This study asked children ages 10-12 about their dream school. They asked them: "Imagine the kind of school you would be eager to study in. What does the school look like? What kind of activities does the ideal school offer?" Each student was asked to write a short story about this school. They could use fantasy in their descriptions. The responses of the 93 students ranged greatly. One student wrote:

> "Now the school has been revised, and it's got everything. The first class is math, and we practice working in a shop. A kind of kiosk has been built outside and everyone gets a chance to be the salesperson. Next, in the Finnish class, we go inside and read the first paragraph. As a surprise, we get to dress up as fairy tale figures. The next class is music, and we go into the woods to play the recorder. We compose songs from the woods, all by ourselves. All the classes have been so much fun that we haven't had a recess until now. In the school yard, I whoosh down a spiral slide, jump on a bouncy castle, swing with lianas, build a sand castle in a large sandbox, and run along a track that requires balance and precision. Then the bell rings and it's time for biology; we examine our own garden and taste different kinds of vegetables. Each class has its own patch of land."

This entry incorporated many of the key elements students were most concerned with: mainly access to the outdoors and combinations of subjects and learning types. Most students wanted to do something fun and active while they learn, and sometimes host class outside. A full breakdown of the categories and resulting concepts can be found in figure 2.8. The study evaluated what the students described in their ideal schools and broke it down into four categories that influence the student at school. The categories include physical well-being and environmental comfort, educational and cultural well-being, socio-emotional well-being and joy of learning, and fantasy and innovation.

This framework helps express the impact of factors that are not easily quantifiable. Elements that impact children's well-being go beyond creating clean classrooms with ideal air quality and lighting. Elements of a space and of the teaching environment that help the student get excited about learning, and thus feel able to be more creative. This idea falls in line with Finland's approach to educational excellence. (Kangas,

1. Initial Coding	Examples
School yard	Football fields, swimming pools, climbing frames, swings, carousels, labyrinths, bouncy castles, gyms, tracks, tennis courts, amusement parts, etc.
School building	Classrooms, halls, lunchrooms, corridors.
Decoration	Plants, comfortable furniture, beautiful and colorful classrooms, lot of windows, lights and spacious rooms, drawings, art on the wall.
Nature	Forest, gardens, hills, flowers, animals, farms, etc.
Topics	Physical education, music, astronomy, cooking. etc.
Learning activities	Playing, studying, competing, giving presentations, gaming, listening to music, dancing, reading, singing, jumping, role playing, using computers, etc.
Instructional tools	Computers, musical instruments, TV's, videos, sport equipment, a big globe.
Recess/break time	Length of recess, forms of activity, etc.
Communal activities	Group work, collaboration, etc.
Homework, vacations	Little homework and tests, long holidays
Freedom of choice	Food, curricula, methods, sports, etc.
Excursions	Night school. half-terms, visits to museums, zoos.
School catering/food	Pizza, hamburgers, pop, healthy food, desserts, several sources, etc.
Fellowship and safety	Friendship, no bullying, no fighting, guards, etc.
Teachers and adults	Kind, nice, agreeable, funny, friendly, strict enough.
Emotional qualifiers	Satisfying, lovely, beautiful, happy, cool, etc.
Fantasy	Time machines, candy or video games factories, learning without effort, getting paid for going to school, etc.

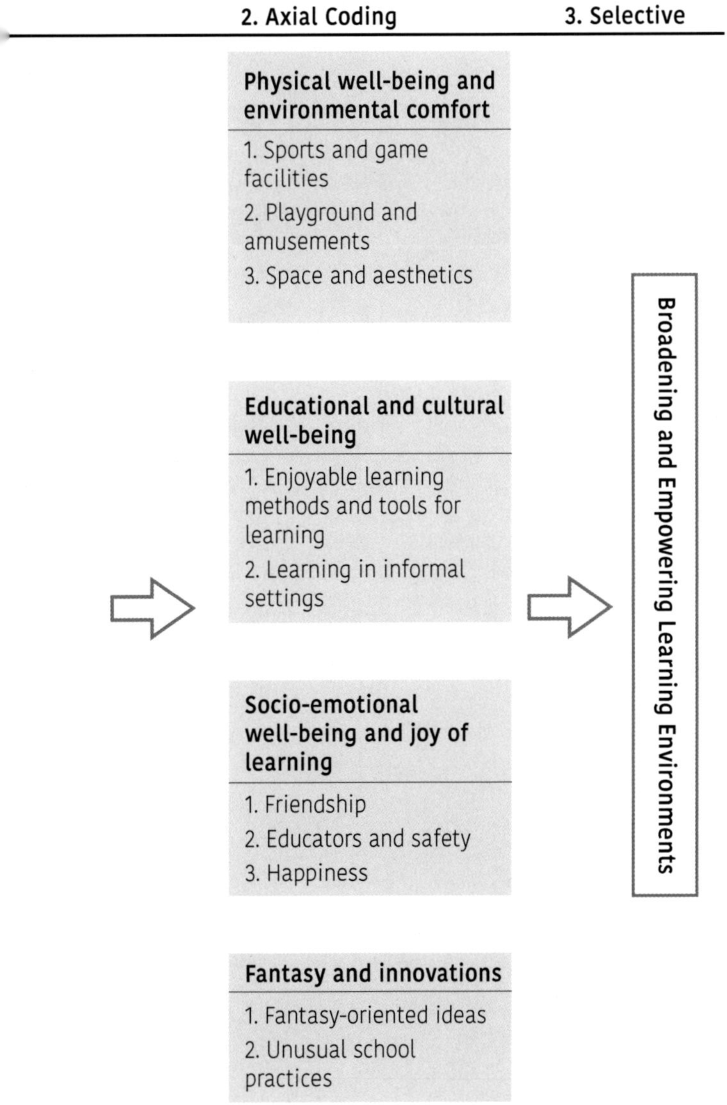

2. Axial Coding   3. Selective

Physical well-being and environmental comfort

1. Sports and game facilities
2. Playground and amusements
3. Space and aesthetics

Educational and cultural well-being

1. Enjoyable learning methods and tools for learning
2. Learning in informal settings

Socio-emotional well-being and joy of learning

1. Friendship
2. Educators and safety
3. Happiness

Fantasy and innovations

1. Fantasy-oriented ideas
2. Unusual school practices

Broadening and Empowering Learning Environments

Advocate + Educate

Figure 2.8 Study Coding process and Categories. Chart based on (Kangas, M., 2010)

M., 2010) states that "educational excellence is about more than statistical averages of student achievement: it also requires that students enjoy learning in school." Also, "there is increasing recognition of the importance of giving children an active role in contributing to learning conditions and involving them in the process of improving and designing learning environments."

These concepts directly correlate to the strategies utilized for creative thinking and promoting environments where children can explore, learn, process information, gain inspiration and express new ideas in a safe manor. Creating healthy environments that not only allow for learning, but also promote creativity and individualization is the next movement in school design. Understanding the balance of each of the many categories listed above will be the key.

When designing a space for learning many factors must be considered. Creating an environment that does not harm the health or hinder the potential of students is critical. This includes designing a space with the appropriate amount of daylight, ventilation, air circulation, views to the outdoors, thermal air quality, etc. These elements which are quantifiable and have direct influence on the health of the occupants. Additionally, the space must be designed to allow flexibility of various degrees based on age. Personalization and adaptability of the spaces and sub-spaces are key to giving students ownership of the space, an element shown to have significant impact on student creativity and learning ability. Creating spaces that promote curiosity and allow for change will give students the space they need to want to be creative.

THE NEW SCHOOL ADVANTAGE

With the growing concern for the state of public school buildings in the United States and the increasing need to remodel or rebuild existing schools, the question of how much a new environment influences student learning arises. Estimates show a need of approximately $197B in capital infusions for school construction, with about $14B spent on construction in 2014. The need for new facilities is clear but the efficacy is not easily measured. A study in Los Angeles, California attempted to measure the significance of moving student populations into new facilities. The study was published in the "Economics of Education Review" by Hashim, Strunk, and Marsh (2018). The project paired new school openings with a reform in their education pedagogy. 131 new schools were added the pool of over 700 public schools in Los Angeles Unified School District (LAUSD) between 2001 and 2008 in an attempt to receive many of the overcrowded schools in the district. Congruently the districts' new "Public School Choice Initiative" was implemented, emphasizing evidence based education tactics. With both of these new elements being implemented simultaneously, the study used standardized test scores of several cohorts to determine success of new schools.

Phase one of this project included strategic placement of new schools as relief for over populated facilities (feeder schools). Schools were placed in the most dense neighborhoods with the highest drop out rates. Because of how the district is divided, the relief schools, built in the densest neighborhoods, were home to the more socioeconomically disadvantages and lower achieving students than their counterparts from the feeder schools (Hanushek, Kain, & Rivkin, 2004 as cited in Hashim, Strunk, and Marsh, 2018). Phase two was the Public School Choice resolution, which aimed to address low performing existing schools as well as the new school pedagogy. This complicated the variables of the study considering with the implementation of a new education system, there was a significant turnover in teachers and staff. Additional turnover was seen with the move to new facilities.

The indicator used to measure students success in the existing and new facilities was the California Standardized Test (CST) and the English Language Arts test (ELA). In the first years of the new schools and new education system there was a drop in scores on both tests in the relief schools. Contributing factors for this include the previously noted population change between the feeder and relief schools, as the relief schools likely serves lower performing schools in denser neighborhoods. This can also be explained by the trend of initial drop in test scores because of the new teaching protocol, increased turnover of teachers and the move to the new facility which can disrupt comfort of young students. This trend only lasted for the first two years of opening the new school. After the second year, the relief schools showed improved test scores, while the feeder schools continued to see scores decrease.

NATURAL ENVIRONMENTS AND CREATIVITY

Modern 21st century environments are typically more immersed in technology and less exposed to natural environments. According to Atchley, et al (2012) there has been a 20% decline in visits to natural parks since 1988 and out of the entire school day only 15-25 minutes are dedicated to outdoor play and sports, and this number continues to decrease. This lack of exposure to nature and decreased physical movement are detrimental to children's physical and mental health and consequently their ability to learn and be creative.

There are many theories promoting increased exposure to nature and the affects of nature on the human psyche. Attention Restorative Theory (ART) explains the positive impact natural environments has on the human attention span. Exposure to natural environments as well as activities in natural settings both replenish the attentional system located in the prefrontal cortex of the brain. Such exposure to nature can help improve concentration needed to learn and perform tasks such as reading or writing. The impacts of exposure to nature on higher level cognitive functions, including creativity, have not yet been explored in depth. However, the research does suggest that because of the restorative affect on the attention span and exposure to varied stimuli, integrating natural environments for informal learning and physical activity in a school setting would help promote creative thinking.

Atchley, et al, 2012 documented a study involving the impacts of exposure to nature on high order cognitive tasks. The experiment tested 56 adults in their late 20's. The Outward Bound organization, a wilderness hiking program in Washington and Alaska, took these adults on a 4-6 day long hike. Using the Remote Associates Test, which tests the cognitive tasks including insight, problem solving and convergent creative reasoning. The participants took the test before and after the hike, showing a 50% increase in score after prolonged exposure to nature. Exposure to nature has been shown to engage a network of areas in the brain which are active during restful introspective thought, known as "default mode." This mode is vital for peak psychosocial health as well as performing many tasks which require the prefrontal lobe. Additionally, interaction with natural environments activates the brain systems involved in divergent thinking, a critical component of creativity.

EXPERIENCING SPACE THROUGH THE SENSES

Architectural theorists have written about tactile, haptic, and sensory rich design for decades. From Kenneth Frampton, to Juhani Pallasmaa, to Peter Zumthor, even neuroscientist Michael Arbib. Each explore how architecture can (or should) be designed for the senses and how the human condition reflects it's surroundings. Architecture is experienced through the senses and through the body, but some spaces are more adequately in tune with the function of the environment than others. Grade schools have a very specific purpose of supporting learning, but more often than not, are build for efficiency, ignoring the specific sensory qualities necessary for learning and creativity (figure 2.9). Designing learning environments for creativity require significant sensitivity towards the senses of children, how they interact and perceive their surroundings. By catering to specific biological sensory needs, these spaces can better serve the occupants and nurture creativity in children.

In the text "A Way of Looking at Things," Peter Zumthor (2006) describes a space from a memory of his childhood,

Figure 2.9 Existing Conditions at Monte Vista Elementary School. Vista, California (photos by author 2017)

"as a time when I experienced architecture without thinking about it. Sometimes I can almost feel a particular door handle in my hand, a piece of metal shaped like the back of a spoon.

...That door handle still seems to me like a special sign of entry into a work of different moods and smalls. I remember the sound of the gravel under my feet, the soft gleam of the waxed oak staircase, I can hear the heavy front door closing behind me as I walk along the dark corridor and enter the kitchen, the only really brightly lit room in the house."

Zumthor explains that the kitchen was not designed to be particularly special, it was typical, by all means of a kitchen. But the way he interacted with it as a child, hyper-aware of the fine details, the way elements felt as he touched them, or the feelings he felt, all remained in his memory.

Similarly in an interview between Peter Zumthor and Juhani Pallasmaa at Aalto University (2018), they discuss the significance of spaces from their childhoods. Both coming from places with lush green environments (Switzerland and Finland, respectively) and significant use of wood in the home, they described similar memories. Pallasmaa described the first spaces in which he felt truly influenced by the space as the small space under the entrance to his house, which was only large enough for him, age 6, the chickens and the family dog to fit. The second space he described was that between the barn and the sauna, a narrow space, also only comfortable for a young child. In the case of both memories, Zumthor and Pallasmaa describe the feeling of being in the space, the texture of the elements they used to touch, the fact that the spaces were too small for adults, but unintentionally appropriately sized for children. In describing the scene, they mention smells, feelings, emotions, tactile experiences, visual tolerances and a specific atmosphere from the perspective of a child.

If children see spaces a certain way, with specific spaces remaining in their memory into adulthood, perhaps these spaces need to be examined. Understanding the elements of a space in which a child is drawn to can help direct the design of spaces for their learning and creativity.

MEMORY AND SPACE

As these architects describe the memory of significant

spaces from their childhood, the question arises of how memory influences the perception of space. Zumthor address memory as influencing perception in multiple ways.

Entering a space for the first time, ones memories of the past influence the way a space is experienced. Because of past experiences, certain visual cues, scents, tactile, sound patterns, etc. will have different significance or call greater attention for one person over another. After the initial visit to the space a new memory will be formed, the space will be mapped in the brain, connecting to other memories and other experiences. Upon returning to a space, the experience may or may not align with the memory recorded in the mind. The atmosphere of the space changes with time. The light shifts with every moment, the temperature of the space changes during the day, the year. The materials weather over the years, the smells change with the seasons. With every return to the environment, the memory changes, adjusts, updates. If the space is visited often, certain elements of it may eventually fall to the background, unnoticed in the conscious mind, until there is a significant change or significant event (Zumthor, 2006).

Memory, in more scientific terms, directly influences ones navigation through space and the recording of that space in the mind. In the article "[why] should architects care about neuroscience?" Michael Arbib (2015) reacts to Zumthor's writing. Arbib recognizes Zumthor's passages on designing from memory as evoking motor imagery as much as visual imagery, evoking action oriented perception (figure 2.10). Thus supporting the ongoing cycle of perception and memory that changes with time and experience.

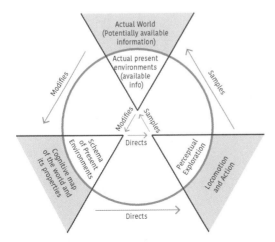

Figure 2.10 Action-Perception Cycle, Diagram by author based on (Arbib, 2015)

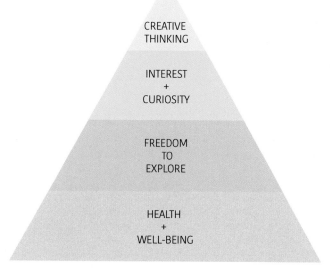

Figure 2.11 Hierarchy of
Environmental Needs for
Creativity

HIERARCHY OF ENVIRONMENTAL
NEEDS FOR CREATIVITY

The built environment can have a dramatic impact on student learning and creativity. Environments influence the way someone feels, their ability to concentrate, and the way they interact with others. This diagram illustrates the hierarchy of needs to promote creative thinking. Prior to addressing further concerns, the architecture must be a healthy environment, both mentally and physically allowing the inhabitant to thrive. Often conditions of outdated, existing schools impede student health with inadequate heating and cooling, lighting and even environmental toxins.

Once the health and well-being of the users are met, the environment can then address the need to promote interest, curiosity and the freedom to explore ideas (figure 2.11). This entails spaces that allow for flexibility of curriculum, pedagogy and scale of work as well as provide an inspirational setting that is comfortable.

The design of learning spaces should not stop at the basic needs. Existing schools should assess the extent to which their facilities fails or succeeds to meet the basic needs of health and well-being for learning, but should not stop there. Interventions to increase a students opportunity and ability to explore and follow their curiosity are endless. The goal of learning environments for creativity is to provide spaces that inspire engagement, and creative thought and activities. This far exceeds the basic health and well-being criteria and do not need to cost more than traditional construction of schools.

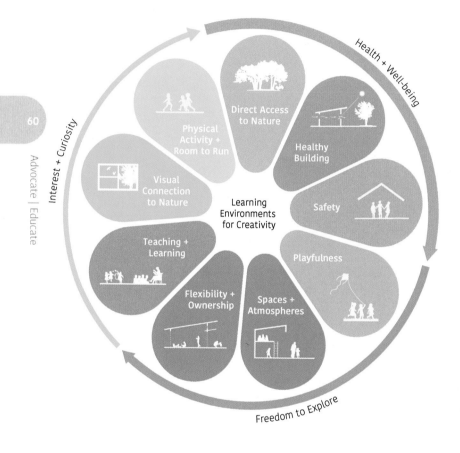

Advocate | Educate

Interest + Curiosity

Health + Well-being

Freedom to Explore

Physical Activity + Room to Run

Direct Access to Nature

Healthy Building

Visual Connection to Nature

Learning Environments for Creativity

Safety

Teaching + Learning

Playfulness

Flexibility + Ownership

Spaces + Atmospheres

Figure 2.12 Nine Principles of
Learning Environments for Creativity

NINE PRINCIPLES OF LEARNING ENVIRONMENTS FOR CREATIVITY

Research to date addressing creating a healthy school environment focuses on creating a space that does not impede the learning abilities of the occupants. This is done through evaluation and finessing of sensorial input. Environmental factors include air quality, thermal comfort, quality of natural and electric light, acoustic conditions, and visual stimuli, etc. But this isn't the entire picture. Other crucial factors include the students' emotional well-being (at home and at school) and how they feel when they go to school, occupy a classroom. The perception of the space is vital to student success.

Illustrated in figure 2.12 is an holistic approach to creativity and well-being of children. Each of the nine principles have architectural and educational implications. Curriculum and pedagogy are integral to student success and creativity. The goal of these strategies is to provide suggestions for the educational framework while emphasizing the architectural opportunities to influence student creativity. The built environment can influence the way teachers and students feel in the space and the way they interact.

DISCUSSION FOR EXISTING SCHOOLS

A single school facility will see countless changes over its lifetime. Changes in curriculum, pedagogy, approach to facility design and design trends. It will remain as new research emerges about how children learn, how to teach the desired outcomes of the era. As the education climate changes, the facility stays standing. The updating of these facilities to match the current educational climate will be a constant cyclical chase.

As we learn more about how the physical environment impacts the health, wellbeing and creativity of its inhabitants, we can strive for adaptability in space, even before that school is up for modernization. Consider the following questions and discuss within your community.

If you are a teacher, consider how to take advantage of your space, indoor and outdoor. Work with your management team and your district to change policies to promote environments that encourage engagement and creativity as the research in this book demonstrates.

If you are a Principal or School District personnel, consider the rules and standards at your school or district. How can positive change be made to improve the experience and learning outcomes of your students along with their overall health and wellbeing?

If you are a designer, consider the reality of the school system, the way a particular school operates as you look into the design of the school. What would have to change in order for the design to work as intended?

If you are in politics or involved in the funding of schools, consider regulations that promote health and wellbeing of its occupants, including regular maintenance and care of all spaces, inside and outside.

How are you utilizing your exciting classroom layout?

> CONSIDER THIS: Classrooms with seating options, groups of different sizes, etc are shown to increase the sense of ownership and autonomy the students feel in the space. Consider a system in which students are able to choose their preferred seating for the week. Consider creating a cozy corner for reading with non-traditional seating.

How do your classrooms look and feel?

> CONSIDER THIS: Research shows that over stimulation to any of the senses can be a detriment on learning and creativity. If the space is cluttered, too hot, too cold, too dark, it can be a problem. Some of these issues can be addressed classroom by classroom, but some may be a result of building systems or overall condition of the facility. Open a dialogue within your school and district about the conditions of classrooms. Consider what can be changed easily by teachers and staff, what is building maintenance and what would require a renovation or building update.

Are you taking advantage of daylight?

> CONSIDER THIS: Exposure to daylight is vital for regulating circadian rhythms. Views to the outdoors, especially with natural settings, have been shown to restore attention deficits. If students are not used to blinds being open, there will be a period of adjustment. Once the novelty of open blinds wears off, student attention and engagement will improve.

Discuss other questions you may have with your peers, your managers, your community and political representatives. Refer to the full color pages in this book for more references on particular topics and visit the website BuildingCreativeSchools.org for continually updated resources to support positive change in schools that support student creativity.

See chapter 3 discussion for more questions to consider when a school is up for renovation or a new school is being designed.

Advocate + Educate

FURTHER READING: CREATIVITY

SCHOLARLY ARTICLES

Barrett, P., Davies, F., Zhang, Y., & Barrett, L. (2015). **The impact of classroom design on pupils' learning: Final results of a holistic, multi-level analysis.** Building and Environment, 89, 118-133. [link]

Chesnokova, O., Subbatsky, E. (2014). **Social creativity in primary-school children: how to measure, develop and accept it**. Procedia - Social and Behavior Sciences, 146, 141-146.

Craft, A. (2001). **An analysis of research and literature on Creativity in Education.** Qualifications and Curriculum Authority. [link]

Dietrich, Arne. (2004) **The Cognitive Neuroscience of Creativity.** Psychonomic Bulletin & Review 11(6): 1011-026. [link]

Fasko, Jr., D. (2001). **Education and Creativity.** (I. Lawrence Erlbaum Associates, Ed.) Creativity Research Journal, 13, 317-327.

Gaier, E., Dellas, M. (1971). **Concept formation and creativity in children.** Theory into Practice, 10(2), 117-123.

Guilford, J.P. (2017). **Can creativity by developed?** Art Education 11(6), 3-7, 14-18.

Hashim, A. K., Strunk, K. O., & Marsh, J. A. (2018). **The new school advantage. Examining the effects of strategic new school openings on student achievement.** Economics of Education Review, 62, 254-266.

Kangas, M. (2010). **Finnish children's views on the ideal school and learning environment.** Learning Environments Research, 13(3), 205-223.

Malinin L.H. (2016). **Creative Practices Embodied, Embedded, and Enacted in Architectural Settings: Toward an Ecological Model of Creativity.** Frontiers in Psychology, 6(1978).

Mellou, E. (1996) **Can Creativity be Nurtured in Young Children?,** Early Child Development and Care, 119(1), 119-130.

Piffer, D. (2012, April 25). **Can creativity be measured? An attempt to clarify the notion of creativity and general directions for future research.** Thinking Skills and Creativity(7), 258-264.

Vandervert, L. R., Schimpf, P. H., & Liu, H. (2007). **How working memory and the cerebellum collaborate to produce creativity and innovation.** Creativity Research Journal, 19(1), 1-18.

MAGAZINE ARTICLES

Hancock, L. (2011, September). **Why Are Finland's Schools Successful?** Smithsonianmag.com. Retrieved from https://www.smithsonianmag.com/innovation/why-are-finlands-schools-successful-49859555/

REPORTS

National Endowment for the Arts (2015). **How creativity works in the brain: insights from a Santa Fe Institute working group.**

VIDEOS

Neuroscience and Design for Special Needs–Learning Environments. Dale, Gallagher, Tarampi, Zandvliet. Academy of Neuroscience for Architecture 2014 https://www.youtube.com/watch?v=t6ThdFtKziI

ANFA Conference(2016). **How Educational Environments Impact Learning.** Dale, Gallagher, Tarampi, Zandvliet. Academy of Neuroscience for Architecture. Retrieved from http://anfarch.org/anfa2016_daleetal/

FURTHER READING: EDUCATION AND INFRASTRUCTURE

REPORTS

Filardo, M., & Vincent, J. M. (2017). **Adequate & Equitable US PK-12 Infrastructure: Priority Actions for Systemic Reform. A Report from the Planning for PK-12 School Infrastructure National Initiative.** 21st Century School Fund.

State of Our Schools (2016) **State of Our Schools: America's K-12 Facilities**. stateofourschools.org

DESIGN GUIDELINES

Tacoma Public Schools (2014). **A vision for the elementary learning environment: guidelines for building planning and design.**

ARUP (2017). **Cities Alive: Designing for urban childhoods.** Received from: https://www.arup.com/publications/research/section/cities-alive-designing-for-urban-childhoods

United States Environmental Protection Agency (2016). **Sensible Guide for Healthier School Renovations: Key Environmental Health Considerations when renovating schools.** https://www.epa.gov/sites/production/files/2016-01/documents/schools_renov_brochure-8_5x11_final.pdf

"...it has become increasingly apparent that children only display creativity when they **want** to and **feel able** to."

- Corpley, A (1995)

SAFETY

Safety in schools is of the utmost importance in education in the United States, with threats and violence prevalent in schools across the country. Safety must be considered across multiple scales. At the campus level, safety is seen as a secure campus, with proper security and supervision to restrict the intruders from intruding the facility.

Safety is also essential at the psychological level. In order for a student to practice creativity, they must feel comfortable in their environment. Sensing environmental safety is critical for students in order to share their ideas and explore thoughts with ease and comfort.

According to neuroscientist John Kounios, a professor of psychology at Drexel University, "Creativity flows from a state of feeling safe or secure. When you feel safe or secure, you can take risks." (Schutle 2015). Kounios explains that any slight, even unconscious threat, prevents someone from feeling safe enough to make a mistake. Due to the intellectual riskiness of creativity, mistakes must be acceptable, and encouraged to promote comprehension.

Before addressing how the physical environment impacts safety in schools it is important to understand the ramifications of trauma and the perception of a safe space on the human brain, and consequently on behavior and learning ability.

TRAUMA AND LEARNING

At the California Coalition of Adequate School Housing (CASH) Conference in 2019 a project was presented regarding the impact of Adverse Childhood Experiences

(ACE's) Scores on human health, wellbeing, and cognitive function (ie, learning and creativity).

The ACE's study was performed by Kaiser Permanente health to understand how trauma influences the longevity of life and overall wellbeing of adults who suffered from childhood trauma. Participants were asked about their exposure to the following circumstances prior to the age of 18:

- Physical, emotional, and/or sexual abuse
- Neglect or abandonment
- Divorce
- Alcoholism or dug addiction in the family
- Family violence
- Poverty, homelessness, lack of food or basic needs
- Family member in prison
- Family member with mental illness

The results showed, of the 17,000 respondents:

- 1 in 4 exposed to 2 categories of ACEs
- 1 in 16 exposed to 4 categories
- 22% were sexually abused as children
- 66% of women experienced abuse, violence, or family strife in childhood
- Woman were 50% more likely than men to have experiences 5 or more ACEs

The study showed that those with experience of 4 or more categories of trauma in childhood experienced increased health risks for alcoholism, drug abuse, depression and suicide attempt by 4 to 12 fold (Felitti et al, 1998).

These trauma factors also have been shown to impact children's ability to learn. The study surveyed families with the Kaiser Permanente health plan (an HMO plan) which in most cases is middle to upper middle class families. Within this demographic, 2,100 children between Kindergarten and 6th grade showed 45% of students were exposed to 1 or more event and 12% had 3 or more adverse events. It was shown that these students had increased rated of academic failure, poor health, sever attendance problems and increased behavior problems at school.

Trauma can present itself in many ways, depending on the child. Some ways it can present are:

- Poor concentration and memory

- Disorientation and confusion
- Socially disconnected and detached
- Depression and mood swings
- Anger, irritability, aggression and verbal or physical outbursts
- Fatigue mentally and physically
- Social withdrawal and isolation

These behaviors can impact not only the child experiencing them, but the entire class. Creating an environment that is physically and emotionally safe will positively impact every student. Many existing schools today allow for little to no autonomy and traditional instructional rigor hinders the students ability to self regulate because they are continually expected to perform and pay attention.

Understanding the potential effect of childhood trauma on the physical, emotional, cognitive and psychosocial health of students brings an additional layer on context that is important in designing facilities for these students. While the context of this book address the learning environments within a school setting on creativity, the student as a whole must be considered. A school must provide a sense of safety to every student. If a student feels unsafe in the classroom, their learning ability will dramatically decrease. The physical environment along with the teaching approach can provide an improved environment which helps students learn to self regulate, self sooth and reengage with their peers, teachers and their own creativity.

CASE STUDY: CALMING CUBBIES

Also presented at the CASH Conference (2019) was a case study demonstrating the power of space on student self regulation and empowerment. Washington Elementary School, an inner-city school in Sacramento, CA was slated to reopen in 2016 after closing in 2014 due to decreased enrollment. The school was re-opened at a STEAM (science, technology, engineering, arts, and mathematics) school and received upgrades to the interior and exterior of the building.

One component of the project was the inclusion of "reading nooks" in every classroom. These were built in casework components at the back of the classroom, visible to the teacher and intended to be fun spaces for the children to do individual activities such as reading.

The students attending this school had high emotional

needs and their ACE's scores were generally high. One teacher did an experiment with her second grade class. After identifying the high emotional needs and the amount of outbursts, distraction and other behavior of disengaged students, the teacher worked with her students to develop a self regulation program.

They developed a system that included leadership roles, silent signals of distress, routine and procedure for re-engagement. Working with the students, they implemented the following systems:

- Upon onset of a stressful feeling or overwhelm the distressed student would signal to the teacher (usually with a hand gesture) that they need to 'tap out". The teacher was able to grant this or deny in the event of a student simply avoiding a task.

- An appointed student leader would touch base with the distressed student asking several questions the class decided on together such as "do you want to talk about it?" and "what happened?"

- If talking to their peer wasn't enough, the student was then able to go into one of the reading nooks/calming cubbies in the back of the classroom for 3-5 minutes. Inside the cubby include diagrams illustrating zones of regulation (figure 2.13), helping students identify their feelings.

- Within the cubby the student had options of self regulating activities, also outlined by the class. Activities included breathing exercises, coloring, drawing or other soothing activities.

This entire process was about 5 minutes and resulted in students returning to class and engaging in the

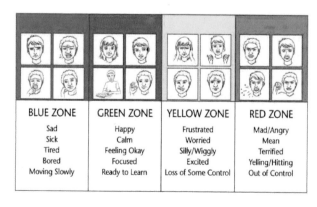

BLUE ZONE	GREEN ZONE	YELLOW ZONE	RED ZONE
Sad	Happy	Frustrated	Mad/Angry
Sick	Calm	Worried	Mean
Tired	Feeling Okay	Silly/Wiggly	Terrified
Bored	Focused	Excited	Yelling/Hitting
Moving Slowly	Ready to Learn	Loss of Some Control	Out of Control

Figure 2.13 Zone of regulation (Iversen, et al, 2019)

learning process rather than remaining checked out and overwhelmed. It also taught the students about naming emotions and self soothing in stressful situation.

Given the success of this experiment, other teachers in the school started implementing these systems, tailoring the rules and regulation options based on their specific group of students. They noticed far fewer outburst and disruptions during class and found the small spaces, though completely visible to the rest of the class provided a space where the children felt saver. The students had choice and autonomy and it resulted in more engaged students learning healthy coping mechanisms at a young age.

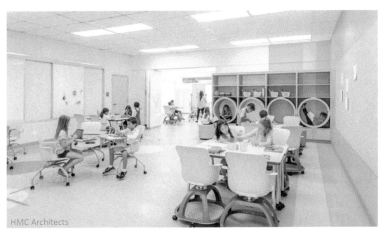

Figure 2.14 Calming Cubbies, Washington Elementary, HMC Architects (Iversen, et al, 2019)

FURTHER READING: SAFETY

SCHOLARLY ARTICLES

Davies, D., Jindal-Snape, D., Collier, C., Digby, R., Hay, P., & Howe, A. (2013). **Creative learning environments in education—A systematic literature review.** Thinking Skills and Creativity, 8, 80-91.

Felitti et al., **"Relationship of Childhood Abuse and Household Dysfunction to Many of the Leading Causes of Death in Adults: The Adverse Childhood Experiences (ACE) Study."** American Journal of Preventative Medacine, Vol. 14 (4). Pages (245-258)

Mellou, E. (1996) **Can Creativity be Nurtured in Young Children?**, Early Child Development and Care, 119(1), 119-130.

Maxwell, L. (2016). **School building condition, social climate, student attendance and academic achievement: a mediation model.** Journal of Environmental Psychology, 46, 206-216,

CONFERENCE PROCEEDINGS

Iversn, A., Godina-Martinez, G., Hankard, N., Buehring, A. (2019). **"Safe Environments: Reconnecting the Cortext to the classroom"**, CASH Annual Conference.

NEWS ARTICLES/INTERVIEWS

Schulte, B. (2015, July 06). **Do these eight things and you will be more creative and insightful, neuroscientists say.** https://www.washingtonpost.com/news/inspired-life/wp/2015/07/06/seven-things-to-do-that-neuroscientists-say-will-enhance-insight-and-boost-creativity/?utm_term=.25628cdbb4ba

Poor air quality, and high levels of carbon dioxide (CO_2) can lead to children getting sick, or worsening asthma symptoms, resulting in the child staying home from school.

HEALTHY BUILDINGS

Healthy buildings are the foundation for the effectiveness of physical environments on student learning, creativity and well-being. Many of the existing facilities occupied today have unacceptable indoor conditions. Poor air quality, high levels of Carbon Dioxide (CO_2) can lead to children getting sick, or worsening asthma symptoms, resulting in the child staying home from school. Thermal comfort is another vital component in how the students perform. Thermal extremes will restrict student engagement and subsequent levels of learning in class.

Sustainability programs, which focus on a holistic approach to building healthy environments, can be used supplementary to the principles outlined in this Toolkit. Sustainable buildings benefit both the users as well as the environment at large. The following pages demonstrate a few of the leading sustainability programs available. Many states have designated sustainability programs for public k-12 schools. This Toolkit is designed to augment these systems, focusing principally on occupant health and resilient systems which additionally serve as educational facilitators.

SUSTAINABILITY RESOURCES

DESIGN GUIDES AND CERTIFICATION SYSTEMS

ASHRAE 2018. **Advanced Energy Design Guide for K-12 School Building: Achieving Zero Energy** https://www.ashrae.org/technical-resources/aedgs/zero-energy-aedg-free-download

Living Building Challenge 3.1: A Visionary Path to a Regenerative Future. https://living-future.org

Collaborative for High Performing Schools (CHPS) https://chps.net/home

LEED for Schools U.S. Green Building Council. https://www.usgbc.org/sites/default/files/leed-and-k12-schools-info-sheet-updated.pdf

International WELL Building Institute. https://www.wellcertified.com/en/explore-standard

Building Research Establishment Environmental Assessment Method (BREEAM) https://www.breeam.com/case-studies/education/

Check your State for specific school sustainability requirements such as:

Washington State: **Washington Sustainability School Protocol.** http://www.k12.wa.us/SchFacilities/Programs/HighPerformanceSchools/WSSP2015EditionCriteria.pdf

FURTHER READING:
HEALTHY BUILDINGS

SCHOLARLY ARTICLES

Barrett, P., Davies, F., Zhang, Y., & Barrett, L. (2015). **The impact of classroom design on pupils' learning: Final results of a holistic, multi-level analysis.** Building and Environment, 89, 118-133.

Duarte, R., Gomes, M.G, Rodrigues, A.M. (2017). **Classroom ventilation with manual opening of windows: findings from a two-year-long experimental study of a Portuguese secondary school.** Building and Environment, 124, 118-129.

Mishra, A.K., Ramgopal, M. (2015). **A comparison of student performance between conditioned and naturally ventilated classrooms.** Building and Environments, 84, 181-188

Sarbu, I., Pacurar, C. (2015). **Experimental and numerical research to assess indoor environment quality and schoolwork performance in university classrooms.** Building and Environments, 93, 141-154.

Stazi, F., Maspi, F., Ulpiani, G., Perna, C.D. (2017). **Indoor air quality and thermal comfort optimization in classrooms developing an automatic system for windows opening and closing.** Energy and Buildings, 139, 732-746.

"Exposure to natural
environments and
performing activities in
nature help replenish the
attentional system."

- Atchley, Stayer, Atchley

DIRECT ACCESS TO
NATURAL ENVIRONMENTS

Natural settings in this context are not limited to lush green settings. The natural environment varies greatly depending on location. Exposure to the natural environment surrounding your school is vital, be it a forest, a desert, a body of water, or dried up lagoon. The key is natural environments, plants, fresh air, patterns provided in nature, etc.

There are numerous theories promoting increased exposure to nature and the affects of nature on the human psyche. Attention Restorative Theory (ART) delineates the positive impact natural environments has on the human attention span. Exposure to natural environments and activities in natural settings replenish the attentional system located in the prefrontal cortex of the brain. Exposure to nature can help improve concentration necessary to learn and perform tasks such as reading or writing. The impacts of exposure to nature on higher level cognitive functions, including creativity, have not yet been explored in depth. However, the research suggests that due to the restorative affect on the attention span and exposure to varied stimuli, integrating natural environments for informal learning and physical activity in a school setting would promote creative thinking.

Research suggests that exposure to nature engages a network of regions in the brain which are active during restful introspective thought, known as "default mode." This mode is vital for peak psychosocial health and for performing tasks which require the prefrontal lobe. Additionally, interaction with natural environments activates the brain systems involved in divergent thinking, a critical component of creativity.

FURTHER READING:
NATURAL ENVIRONMENTS

SCHOLARLY ARTICLES

Atchley RA, Strayer DL, Atchley P (2012) **Creativity in the Wild: Improving Creative Reasoning through Immersion in Natural Settings.** PLoS ONE 7(12):e51474.

Barrett, P., Davies, F., Zhang, Y., & Barrett, L. (2015). **The impact of classroom design on pupils' learning: Final results of a holistic, multi-level analysis.** Building and Environment, 89, 118-133.

Gilavand, A., Espidkar, F., & Gilavand, M. (2016). **Investigating the Impact of Schools' Open Space on Learning and Educational Achievement of Elementary Students.** International Journal of Pediatrics, 4(4), 1663- 1670.

Kweon, B.S., Ellis, C., Lee, J., Jacobs, K. (2017). **The link between school environments and student academic performance.** Urban Forestry & Greening, 23, 35-43.

The Outdoor Classroom Project (2015) **The Outdoor Classroom.** Retrieved from http:// outdoorclassroomproject.org/about/ the-outdoor-classroom/

VIDEOS

Behling, Stefan. (2016) **Architecture and the Science of the Senses.** TEDx Talks. TEDxGoodenoughCollege. Retrieved from https://www.youtube.com/ watch?v=FbfPWalO_ss

"Physical activity has a positive influence on memory, concentration and classroom behavior."

- Strong, et al (2005)

PHYSICAL ACTIVITY + ROOM TO RUN

In the United States children typically have less than half an hour of recess every day, and that number is continuing to decrease. Increasing exercise and play to at least one hour per day has been shown to decrease depression and anxiety and improve overall mental and physical health (Strong, et al, 2005).

Physical health and mental health are directly reliant on one another. Physical exercise promotes the production of hormones in the brain and body associated with increased focus, attention, excitement, happiness, etc. Interspersing exercise throughout the day also gives the mind a break from more conventional classroom learning tasks. Altering the environment helps relieve mental fatigue.

In Finland, a country known for its education system, students have a 15 minute break to go outside and run around every 45 minutes of instruction or in class activity. This gives the brain time to digest the information presented during the class sessions (Walker, T., 2017).

FURTHER READING: PHYSICAL ACTIVITY

ARTICLES

Strong, W. B., Malina, R. M., Blimkie, C. J. R., Daniels, S. R., Dishman, R. K., Gutin, B., ... Trudeau, F. (2005). **Evidence Based Physical Activity for School-age Youth**. The Journal of Pediatrics, 146(6), 732–737. https://doi.org/10.1016/j.jpeds.2005.01.055

Withagen R, Caljouw S.R. (2017) **Aldo van Eyck's Playgrounds: Aesthetics, Affordances, and Creativity.** Frontiers in Psychology. 8(1130).

REPORTS/WHITE PAPER

Playworld (2014). **The role of recess in academics and whole child development.** The Play Report, vol. 2.

Breithecker, D. (2009). **Bodies in motion, brains in motion.** Federal Institute on the Development of Posture and Exercise. https://www.aquestdesign.ca/docs/45-066-02_V01_EN_Bodies_in_Motion-120602.pdf

NEWS ARTICLES/INTERVIEWS

Walker, T. (2017, June 17). BBC Interview: Timothy D. Walker, author of **"Teach Like Finland."** Retrieved January 29, 2018, from http://taughtbyfinland.com/bbc-world-news-interview/

Views to nature promote relaxation, expansion and increase attention and creativity

- Byoung-Suk Kweona

VISUAL CONNECTION TO NATURE

Views to nature and views beyond the confined classroom help improve creativity. In attention to the restorative qualities of natural environments, the sky and green landscapes, extended views aid in expanding the conceptual attention on an individual. According to Professor Kounior of Drexel University, increasing the visual field influences the way the brain focuses attention. In larger spaces, the visual attention expands to fill the space and consequentially expands the conceptual attention, essentially opening the mind to new ideas (Schutle 2015).

Vision is considered the most important sense involved in the perception of space. The physical eye can only see light and color, but the brain translates that input into significant information. This is linked to several other senses, including balance and movement. Visual information has a dramatic impact on ones sense of self, and mood. Ones mood and even health change based on the color of a space, the quality and color of the light. The human body regulates hormones and endorphins based on light, natural and artificial. Children are particularly sensitive to their surroundings. Creating a visually diverse environment is key for children to feel comfortable and inspired. Views to nature and the environment beyond the classroom allows the eyes and mind to expand focus while increasing daylight.

FURTHER READING: VISUAL CONNECTION TO NATURE

BOOKS

Berger, J. (2008). **Ways of seeing**. London: Penguin.

ARTICLES

Barrett, P., Davies, F., Zhang, Y., & Barrett, L. (2015). **The impact of classroom design on pupils' learning: Final results of a holistic, multi-level analysis.** Building and Environment, 89, 118-133.

Heschong, L., Wright, R, Okura, S. (1999). **Daylighting and productivity: elementary school studies.** Consumer Behavior and Non-Energy Effects, 8(149).

Tennessen, C.M., Cimprich, B. (1995) **Views to nature: Effects on attention.** Journal of Environmental Psychology, 15(1), 77-85.

NEWS ARTICLES/INTERVIEWS

Schulte, B. (2015, July 06). **Do these eight things and you will be more creative and insightful, neuroscientists say.** Retrieved April 03, 2018, from https://www.washingtonpost.com/news/inspired-life/wp/2015/07/06/seven-things-to-do-that-neuroscientists-say-will-enhance-insight-and-boost-creativity/?utm_term=.25628cdbb4ba

VIDEOS

Behling, Stefan. (2016) **Architecture and the Science of the Senses.** TEDx Talks. TEDxGoodenoughCollege. Retrieved from https://www.youtube.com/watch?v=FbfPWalO_ss

"Schools are supposed to be welcoming; like a second home to students and building conditions are directly linked to a student's engagement and willingness to learn."

- Port Angeles High School Junior, 2018

TEACHING + LEARNING

The built environment impacts both the teacher and the student. Student creativity and learning ability is directly influenced by the enthusiasm and ability of the teacher, their approach to teaching and the students' learning styles. The architecture is the foundation for the activities that happen within. The built environment is built around the demands of the pedagogy; on the other hand the physical space can help moderate the teaching methods.

Current pedagogy is shifting towards project based learning instead of focusing on information delivery and regurgitation via worksheets, this approach focuses on idea exploration. Meaning that curriculum, lectures and homework all change. This type of project-based learning is often used in Kindergarten and is lost in higher grade levels (Resnick, M.,Robinson, K., 2017.) Retaining this process in higher grade levels will encourage creative thinking and help the students build the habit of problem solving.

The architecture can stimulate creativity by providing spaces that encourage divergent thinking: exploring how things are made and generating as many ideas as possible. These environments are highly flexible, allowing multiple learning settings to occur in the same space, peaking student interest and engagement through different teaching methods and exercises.

FURTHER READING:
TEACHING + LEARNING

BOOKS

Resnick, M., & Robinson, K. (2017). **Lifelong kindergarten: cultivating creativity through projects, passion, peers, and play.** Cambridge, MA: The MIT Press.

Cannon Design, VS Furniture, & Bruce Mau Design. (2010). **The Third Teacher.** New York: Abrams.

SCHOLARLY ARTICLES

Brock, L. L., Nishida, T. K., Chiong, C., Grimm, K. J., & Rimm-Kaufman, S. E. (2008). **Children's perceptions of the classroom environment and social and academic performance: A longitudinal analysis of the contribution of the Responsive Classroom approach.** Journal of School Psychology, 2, 129-149.

Corpley, A. J. (1995). **Fostering creativity in the classroom: General principles.** In M. Runco (Ed.), The creativity research handbook Vol. 1 (p.83-114). Cresskill, NJ: Hampton Press.

Esquivel, G.B. (1995). **Teacher behaviors that foster creativity.** Educational Psychology Review, 7(2), 185-202.

Lin, Y.S., (2011). **Fostering Creativity through education: a conceptual framework of creative pedagogy.** Creative Education, 2(3), 149-115.

Poysa, S, et al. (2018). **Variation in situation-specific engagement among lower secondary school students.** Learning and Instruction, 53, 64-73.

MAGAZINE ARTICLES

Rasti, I. (2018, January 11). **How Creative Teaching Improves Students' Executive Function Skills.** The Creative Post. Retrieved February 13, 2018, from http://www.creativitypost.com

"The desks and chairs are easy to move which has made learning easier. We no longer have bulky furniture that is hard to move, instead we have furniture that moves with a breeze. The chairs don't hurt my back and we finally have a room to move around. I wish every class was like this."

- HS Student, Orange County Pilot Project, 2016

FLEXIBILITY + OWNERSHIP

Individualization and stimulation results varied with age groups, accordingly. In younger children, greater diversity of learning environments is desirable. Irregularly shaped classrooms allow for study nooks and areas for varied physical environments that allow students with different learning styles to thrive. These spaces can be customized to provide students with a strong sense of ownership. However, this level of individualization also increases visual stimuli.

Younger students respond well to higher levels of stimuli and more complexity in the room design. Older students performed better in visually simplified classrooms with less individualization, but with a regular shaped room and less visual stimuli than in the classrooms for younger children. Additionally, it was found that exhibiting student work throughout the school, and in the classrooms, helped encourage ownership and boosted self-esteem of the students at all ages.

Research in visual stimulation shows that some use of color on an accent wall will create a positive mood in the classroom, but too much, or too vibrant color will tip the stimuli scale to excessive and distracting. Both under-stimulating and over-stimulating rooms performed poorly in this study.

Flexibility + Ownership

Flexibility + Ownership

FURTHER READING:
FLEXIBILITY + OWNERSHIP

ARTICLES

Rodgers, D.B. (1998). **Supporting autonomy in young children**. Young Children, 53(3), 75-80.

REPORTS

Breithecker, D. (2009). **Bodies in motion, brains in motion.** Federal Institute on the Development of Posture and Exercise. https://www.aquestdesign.ca/docs/45-066-02_V01_EN_Bodies_in_Motion-120602.pdf

VIDEOS

PK Yonge DRS. (2012). **Kids LOVE new school!** [Video]. Retrieved from https://www.youtube.com /watch?v=NT7Sy9APTPo&feature=youtu.be

Spaces + Atmospheres

"Children actually experience all of their surroundings: room, wallpaper, furniture, colors, and even the air in the classroom. All this can either be friendly or oppressive."

- Felix Durach

SPACES + ATMOSPHERES

Varied learning exercises, learning styles and teaching styles require diverse set of spaces. The atmosphere of a place sets the tone for what activities take place. This is especially key for younger children, who, in general, inhabit spaces designed and sized for adults. Learning environments should accommodate those using the space: the children.

Children, like adults, experience their surroundings through all of their senses. While many adults become desensitized to certain environmental conditions, children tend to be more sensitive and experience their surroundings differently. This must be taken into consideration depending on what age group will inhabit the school.

The atmosphere of a room sets the stage for behaviors and tasks which occur within it. Depending on the context, the environment can promote quiet, individual work to messy and noisy group activities. This principle is tied closely to the previous "Flexibility and Ownership" in that certain conditions will promote students take ownership over the space, adapting it to their needs while others will dictate a more rigidity.

FURTHER READING:
FLEXIBILITY + OWNERSHIP

ARTICLES

Barrett, P., Davies, F., Zhang, Y., & Barrett, L. (2015). **The impact of classroom design on pupils' learning: Final results of a holistic, multi-level analysis.** Building and Environment, 89, 118-133.

Davies, D., Jindal-Snape, D., Collier, C., Digby, R., Hay, P., & Howe, A. (2013). **Creative learning environments in education—A systematic literature review.** Thinking Skills and Creativity, 8, 80-91.

Kangas, M. (2010). **Finnish children's views on the ideal school and learning environment.** Learning Environments Research, 13(3), 205-223.

Richardson, C., & Mishra, P. (2018). **Learning environments that support student creativity: Developing the SCALE.** Thinking Skills and Creativity, 27, 45-54.

VIDEOS

ANFA Conference(2016). **How Educational Environments Impact Learning.** Dale, J. Academy of Neuroscience for Architecture. Retrieved from http://anfarch.org/anfa2016_daleetal/

Playfulness is often something associated with childhood, something one grows out of. But, in fact, play is an important part of creativity and learning.

PLAYFULNESS

When addressing creativity in children (of any age), playfulness, imagination and curiosity must be addressed. Children learn through experimenting, following their curiosity and playing with objects, boundaries and their own mechanics. Playfulness occurs at many levels including a physical and mental level. A child can be playful physically, experimenting with something through all of the senses. They can also play with other children in the classroom, the playground, etc. Playfulness can also be purely in thought, exploring ideas in the mind with a lightness of mood. In "Play, playfulness, creativity and innovation" Bateson, P., and Martin, P. (2013) outline criteria for "Play" as the following:

- The behavior is spontaneous and rewarding to the individual,

- It is intrinsically motivated and its performance is a goal in itself,

- The behavior occurs in a protected context when the player is neither ill nor stressed,

- The behavior is incomplete or exaggerated relative to the non-playful behavior (in adults)

- It is performed repeatedly

The act of playing and the state of mind denoted as playful are similarly impacted by the atmosphere, or mood of the space and the arrangement of the space.

FURTHER READING:
PLAYFULNESS

BOOKS

Bateson, P., & Martin, P. (2013). **Play, playfulness, creativity and innovation.** Cambridge: Cambridge University Press. [link to article 2014]

Russ, S. W. (2014). **Pretend Play in Childhood: Foundation of Adult Creativity.** Washington: American Psychological Association.

ARTICLES

Withagen R, Caljouw S.R. (2017) **Aldo van Eyck's Playgrounds: Aesthetics, Affordances, and Creativity.** Frontiers in Psychology. 8(1130).

REPORTS/WHITE PAPER

Playworld (2014). **The role of recess in academics and whole child development.** The Play Report, vol. 2.

Breithecker, D. (2009). **Bodies in motion, brains in motion.** Federal Institute on the Development of Posture and Exercise. https://www.aquestdesign.ca/docs/45-066-02_V01_EN_Bodies_in_Motion-120602.pdf

NOTES

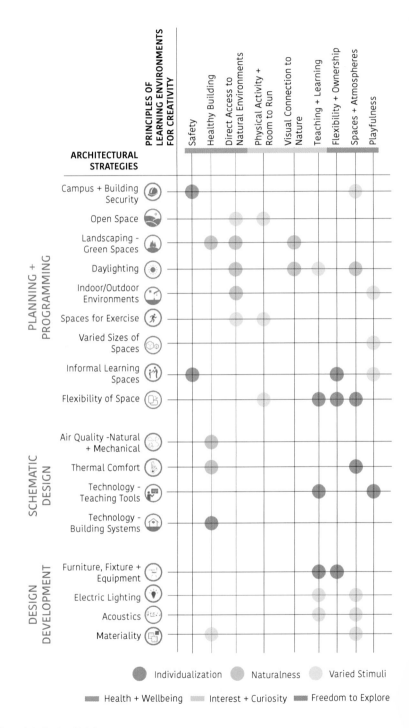

Figure 3.1 Design Matrix

3

PROJECT INTEGRATION

The following section outlines best practice strategies for architectural components of school design, organized to fit the typical design-bid-build trajectory. When delivery methodologies are used, such as Construction Management at Risk or even Design-Build, the following design strategies are still to be implemented as early as possible. These concepts are not limited to type of delivery for architectural services.

As previously outlined, the project goals should be discussed and agreed upon by the entire project team, including the site principal and School District education and design teams. These architectural strategies fit within the holistic approach address by the Nine Principles of Learning Environments for Creativity. Depending on the project goals, state of existing facilities, extent of scope and available budget, some strategies will become higher priority.

Figure 3.1 shows the translation of the Nine Principles of Learning Environments for Creativity; the psychological and systematic impacts on child learning and creativity, to the architectural and design elements of a school. This section will explain each of these architectural strategies as they apply to creativity and provide examples of best practice for design. This is not a once size fits all, every school and population is unique. Understanding the impacts of each architectural strategy can help inform the project priorities to deliver the highest positive impact on student and teacher wellbeing, learning and creativity.

Project Integration

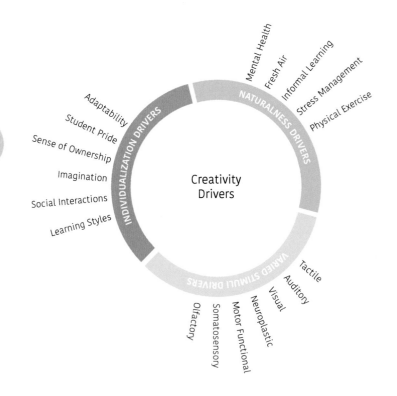

Figure 3.2 Cognitive and Environmental
Drivers for Creativity

COGNITIVE AND ENVIRONMENTAL DRIVERS FOR CREATIVITY

As seen in the researched in chapter 2, there are numerous factors that impact student learning and creativity. However, given the state of schools, any existing conditions, scope of work, timeline, budgetary constraints, etc, it is rarely possible to integrate all of these concepts into a single project. Integration will look different in every school and the conditions of the school and needs of the specific students must be at the forefront of the design discussion.

Figure 3.2 shows the linkage between the architectural themes and the cognitive drivers for creativity. The study in England (Barrett, Davies, Zhang, & Barrett, 2015) in chapter 2, outlines 3 major categories of architectural elements and defines them as follows:

- **Naturalness** includes natural and electric light, noise level, temperature and control of thermal comfort, air quality (based on CO_2 levels present) adjust-ability of air exchange, and links to nature; visually and directly.

- **Individualization** focuses on ownership and flexibility of the space. How a space can be customized, rearranged, and the level of connectivity to the rest of the school.

- **Stimulation** concentrates on sensorial information within the learning space, ranging from complexity of the room and layout, to the color choice, to the amount of decoration or excess noise.

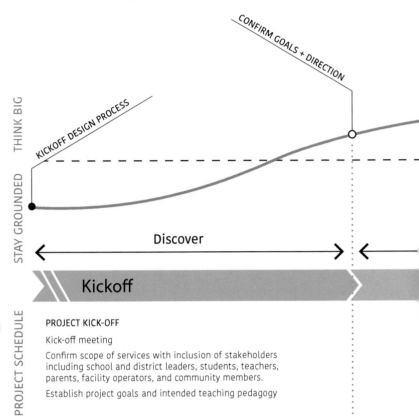

THINK BIG

STAY GROUNDED

KICKOFF DESIGN PROCESS

CONFIRM GOALS + DIRECTION

Discover

Kickoff

PROJECT SCHEDULE

PROJECT KICK-OFF

Kick-off meeting

Confirm scope of services with inclusion of stakeholders including school and district leaders, students, teachers, parents, facility operators, and community members.

Establish project goals and intended teaching pedagogy

REFER TO TOOLKIT

THE ROLE OF CREATIVITY

Discuss and encourage education pedagogies directed towards nurturing creativity with the client/school. Use the toolkit to show evidence of the benefits of designing spaces for creativity.

Involve the users (teachers, students, parents) to establish the short and long term goals for the school.

Document needs of the students and intentions of teaching pedagogy.

Figure 3.3 Toolkit Timeline
Integration (cont. next page)

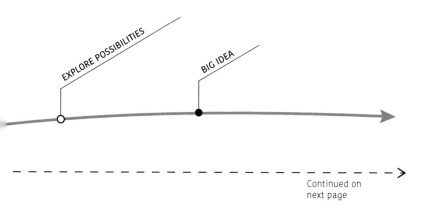

Continued on
next page

Explore

Planning + Programming

EVALUATE EXISTING FACILITY

Site Analysis + Infrastructure inventory

Document existing conditions

Determine project concept

Define school programming - existing to remain, alterations
and new program

Establish scope of services and project timeline

DETERMINING COURSE OF ACTION

Based on existing conditions and budget, determine which elements need the
most attention.

Consult toolkit for best course of action depending on established needs and
what improvements will have the greatest impact on student creativity and
well-being.

Refer to toolkit for inspiration and ideas as well as design specifics

ARCHITECTURAL STRATEGIES

Campus + Building Security

Open Space

Landscaping - Green Spaces

Daylighting

Indoor/Outdoor Environments

Spaces for Exercise

Varied Sizes of Spaces

Informal Learning Spaces

Flexibility of Space

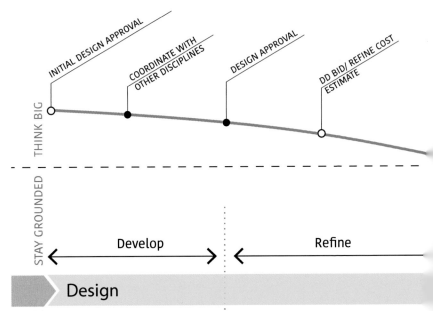

Project Integration

THINK BIG

INITIAL DESIGN APPROVAL

COORDINATE WITH OTHER DISCIPLINES

DESIGN APPROVAL

DD BID/ REFINE COST ESTIMATE

STAY GROUNDED

Develop

Refine

Design

PROJECT SCHEDULE

SCHEMATIC DESIGN

Develop feasible design concepts

Explore design options

Initial cost analysis

DESIGN DEVELOPMENT

Refine project design

Coordinate project details with other disciplines

Develop project specifications

REFER TO TOOLKIT

DEVELOPING FOR CREATIVITY

Consult toolkit for best practice design optimizing learning environments that support creativity and well-being.

Refer to toolkit for specific strategies to improve the users experience of the space.

REFINING FOR CREATIVITY

Refer to toolkit for preferred design elements to nurture creativity and student well-being.

Adjust design features according to budget while retaining as many elements that support creativity and occupant well-being.

ARCHITECTURAL STRATEGIES

Air Quality - Natural + Mechanical

Thermal Comfort

Technology - Teaching Tools

Technology - Building Systems

Building Porosity

ARCHITECTURAL STRATEGIES

Furniture, Fixture + Equipment

Electric Lighting

Acoustics

Materiality

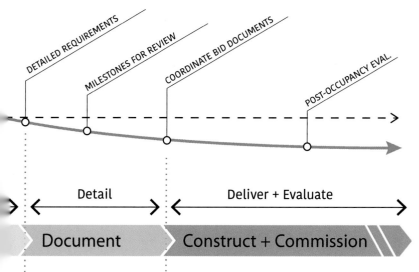

DETAILED REQUIREMENTS

MILESTONES FOR REVIEW

COORDINATE BID DOCUMENTS

POST-OCCUPANCY EVAL.

Detail	Deliver + Evaluate

Document ⟩ Construct + Commission

CONSTRUCTION DOCUMENTS

Prepare construction documents

Permitting procedures

Jurisdiction approval process

BIDDING + CONSTRUCTION

Bidding + addendum

Construction administration

Project closeout

Post occupancy evaluation of design systems

DETAILING FOR CREATIVITY

Integrate evidence based design throughout the project.

Verify that project details support the big picture of creating spaces to nurture creativity as outlines in the project goals.

EVALUATE LESSONS LEARNED

Review level of success of project goals post-occupancy. Determine which elements could be executed more effectively next time.

Take notes in the Toolkit of project failures and successes and ideas for future projects.

Project Integration

Figure 3.4 Hierarchy of
Environmental Needs for Creativity

Project Integration

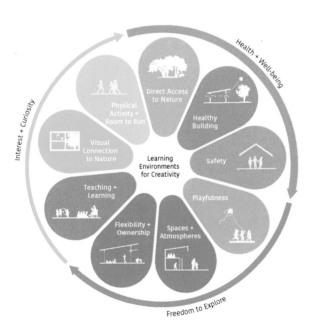

Figure 3.5 Nine Principles of
Learning Environments for Creativity

KICK-OFF | DISCOVER

During the Kick-off of a project, establish the role of creativity within the project goals. If the project is a renovation or modernization of an existing school, determine the elements of the facility which need the most improvement, and which components can have the biggest impact on the student's experience of the space.

Figure 3.4 and 3.5, also seen in chapter 2, shows the hierarchy of needs for creativity in respect to the physical environment and the corresponding principles for creativity. This shows that the foundation for a healthy school that promotes creativity starts with basic comfort. While this may seem obvious, many schools across the country do not meet these needs, as seen in the student testimonies in chapter 2.

The effectiveness of implementing this holistic approach is reliant on a collaborative environment. Involving as many users as possible including students, teachers, staff, and parents to evaluate the direction and goals of the school will strengthen the outcome. Integrating the design team and bringing on consultants early on in the project will also increase the efficiency of the workflow.

DISCUSSION

How do you anticipate the classrooms being used?

> CONSIDER THIS: Classrooms with flexible/mobile furniture encourage more student interaction and promote ownership of the space, and as a result students will be more engaged and enthusiastic about what they are learning.

Are you changing the curriculum or teaching approach?

> CONSIDER THIS: Gearing the curriculum and pedagogy towards project-based learning has been shown to improve student involvement and willingness to learn. Depending on the pathway, this may be more or less appropriate, however, direct hands-on learning can be successful at many scales. Consider pathways appropriate to your community at large.
>
> Project based learning also offers flexibility based on the individual students base knowledge and learning process, allowing students to learn different paces.

Are you introducing any new programs or pathways with this renovation/new school?

> CONSIDER THIS: Larger, flexible multi-purpose spaces can be used for makers spaces. Consider having a multi-purpose space near a classroom or storage space that houses "maker" tools and supplies.
>
> Expanded pathway options often require specialized equipment. As these pathways change over time, a larger, adaptable space can be changed and equipment removed/replaced with more ease, without significant building modifications.

DISCUSSION

How do you anticipate the classrooms being used?

CONSIDER THIS: Classrooms with flexible/mobile furniture encourage more student interaction and promote ownership of the space, and as a result students will be more engaged and enthusiastic about what they are learning.

How does your school engage with the local community? How can you increase this involvement and engagement with parents, with local businesses, with neighbors, with local colleges?

CONSIDER THIS: Schools with higher community involvement from parents and family to the community at large will create a sense of ownership and pride with the school. By allowing the community to participate and engage with the school, they will feel a personal investment in the success of the students.

Take into the account the local community supporting the school, this can include businesses and other neighboring communities. The goal is to integrate the school with their context, create more connections and opportunities, rather than creating a silo. This is particularly important to support schools in low income neighborhoods or where traditional support from is difficult to achieve.

For existing schools: **How do you currently utilize outdoor space? Are classes taught outside? Do you see potential to expand the classrooms outside?**

For new schools: **How do you envision outdoor space being used? Are classes taught outside? Do you see potential to expand the classroom outside?**

CONSIDER THIS: Teaching outdoors is an effective way to change the learning environment, increase engagement and promote hands on learning for a particular activity. Exposure to the elements and natural environments promotes attention restoration and a multitude of other health benefits.

If you are in an urban setting, this may happen by engaging local parks and gardens or utilizing rooftop or internal courtyard spaces, depending on your site.

Project Integration

4

DESIGN STRATEGIES

The design strategies in this section range from big-picture concepts to specific details and fixture selection. While each have specific information and needs associated with them, many of the strategies overlap and blend together. The more integrated the project, the more blurred each of the strategies will become. The success of the project relies on interdisciplinary participation and active listening to the needs of the school, students, teachers and clients.

The strategies are outlines based on when each task is typically presented in a project. The earlier each item is discussed, the more successfully it will be implemented. Some strategies may require additional consultants and expertise be brought on earlier in design development or schematic design in an integrated approach.

INDUSTRY INVOLVEMENT

In order to test the relevance and usability of the principles and strategies developed in this project, a focus group was held with eight San Diego, CA architects whose expertise include grade school design. Each architect was selected for their expertise and leadership in school design in San Diego. Prior to the workshop, each attendee was supplied with background information about the project and the design principles in development.

During the workshop each architect provided feedback on their experience implementing each of the principles in real life projects. This was to gauge how clients and the community realistically welcome or resist different design ideas.

PERCEPTION OF INFLUENTIAL ARCHITECTURAL ELEMENTS

According to the responses during the exercise and the discussion that followed the primary environmental concerns regarding nurturing creativity came down to a few basic elements. These elements play a vital role in making a space comfortable. One attendee told a story during the discussion that demonstrated the affect of discomfort on learning. His story:

> In a college course, the teacher asked all of her students to stand up during the lecture. She asked for everyone to balance on one leg as she proceeded to give the lecture. She continues giving the lecture as she would in any other class. After a minute or so students began to wobble one their standing leg, trying to keep balance and not fall. The instructor

continued for another minute or so as students continued to struggle balancing. She then instructs everyone to stop and return to standing on both feet. She then quizzed the class on the material she had just covered. In chronological order, most students were about to answer the first few questions about that covered material. As she got further into the lecture, it was harder for students to recall the information, until very few were able to recall anything covered during the most difficult stages of balancing.

This exercise demonstrated the power of comfort on learning, even simply recalling information, not complicated problem solving or creativity. As the students struggled to balance on one foot, their mental energy shifted from the instructor and course information and eventually completely focused on staying in an upright position on one foot. The higher the level of discomfort, the harder it is for a student to pay attention, recall information. Higher level cognitive processes such as creative problem solving would be impossible under these conditions. Balancing on one foot is a simple example of discomfort, however there are many elements of the environment which influence physical, and mental, comfort. These were the items of the highest concern during the focus group.

The primary role of a classroom is to support learning. This most basic requirements include student safety, mentally, emotionally and physically, as well as thermally and acoustically comfortable. These are the foundation, if these requirements are not met, nothing else will make a difference. This feedback aligns with the literature review in chapter two and the developed hierarchy of needs with health and well-being as the base.

Architectural elements which were deemed most significant for basic comfort include:

- **Building Safety:** Physical and mental safety were discussed as highest priority. This includes campus security from outside threats as well as psychological safety in a given cohort and space. If a student feels even remotely threatened, learning becomes increasingly challenging and creativity is not a possibility.

- **Thermal Comfort:** Learning environments need to be a comfortable temperature and humidity for various activities. Ability to change the environments increase comfort and perception of the temperature/humidity. This can be done through mechanical thermal control (thermostat) in each space or manual controls including operable windows and ceiling fans to help change the room conditions as needed. Different activities require varied thermal conditions.

- **Air Quality:** Air quality is significant, especially in older schools that require modernization. Mechanical systems are among the largest components of modernizations and renovation projects, as they fail or under perform by the time a school is considered for an update. Poor air circulation or toxic air quality dramatically impacts students, sometimes even resulting in students going home sick and increase asthmatic episodes.

- **Acoustics:** Acoustics are a fundamental requirement for learning and creativity. A classroom, or other learning environments require acoustic conditions for instruction, quiet individual work, and large group work which may be a higher volume. If the room does not adequately manage this range in volumes and tasks the student will either be unable to properly hear the teacher, or the room may be too noisy to focus on a task at hand. Acoustic treatments are relatively easy to add and adjust in exciting facilities with surface treatments for disbursement and dampening of sound. If the facility construction is inadequate and sounds travel from one part of the building to another, this becomes more challenging to retrofit, but still possible.

- **Lighting**: The amount and quality of the light in the space directly influences a students ability to learn. If the room is too dark, this causes stress to the eyes and makes it difficult to understand read materials or even tasks. Over-lighting is also distracting, but far less common, especially in existing facilities. The most common form of over-lighting is from daylight glare, which can be managed through shading of direct daylight. Color temperature and type of lighting (florescent, incandescent or LED) can also impact light quality, some types of lighting can cause headaches and ocular fatigue in students and teachers.

If these items are not addressed or executed properly, the learning environment will fail. As the antidote previously demonstrated, if a student is somehow physically uncomfortable, learning will be minimized.

This group of architects involved in this discussion

focused on these items over any others. They acknowledged that things can be done above and beyond this to encourage engagement and a sense of ownership and supported variety spaces, however due to the state of schools, the fundamentals listen above consumed the majority of the conversation.

SOURCES OF RESISTANCE

While the fundamental healthy environment factors mentioned above were undeniably the priority, they also seemed to receive the least amount of resistance. Nuances of each item have a certain level of resistance, for instance, the selection of ventilation systems as they are perceived to be more expensive or more difficult to maintain. However, the over-arching principle is supported. Strategies which do receive push back, include informal learning spaces, blended indoor/outdoor environments, flexibility and technology and materiality. Much of the push back stemmed from the perceived idea that informal spaces, or flexible spaces or indoor/outdoor environments were creating redundant and expensive space. Below are some of the highlighted points regarding resistance:

- **Campus Security**: While everyone supports a safe and secure campus, the primary obstacle observed was teachers and staff within the school propping doors open so they can leave campus or run to their car and return without going through the primary entry, which is often a longer path of travel. This is a minor case of resistance, but breaks the security of the building that outsiders can take advantage of.

  Another obstacle with campus security is the balance between hyper secure and an open and engaging environment. Typical protocol in California includes a ten foot chain linked fence at the perimeter of the campus. This is not always effective and is unattractive and reminiscent of a prison, however it is an inexpensive "solution." The workshop participants suggest more creative solutions for campus security including using the building as a fence where possible or if budget allows, designing a more aesthetically pleasing fence.

- **Informal Learning Spaces, Indoor/Outdoor Environments, and Varied Spaces**: These strategies, though all unique received the same overall source of resistance: misunderstanding of importance. Often times, clients will express that these types of spaces cost too much or are seen as a redundant use of space. These spaces are typically seen as addition programmed space beyond the conventional classroom. They are often seen as unnecessary. School projects with higher budgets and larger sites are generally more open to integrating these elements into the design. This shows the need to educate everyone involved about the importance of these spaces for children's learning and creativity as well as demonstrate how to integrate them into projects of all sizes and budgets. These spaces can often become the circulation or become part of the classroom spaces.

- **Furniture, Fixture, Equipment and Materiality:** The number one source of resistance on these items is from the perspective of maintenance and operations staff. With new technology, new materials, new furniture, the care and cleaning is changing. School personnel are used to cleaning and maintaining equipment and facilities in a certain way. The workshop uncovered several anecdotes of maintenance staff using old cleaning techniques on new flooring systems, essentially ruining the floor surface. Other examples were given regarding misunderstanding of new protocol for upkeep or newer or different systems. This shows the need to educate the users on the benefits of these systems and training them in how to maintain the equipment, fixtures and materials. Similar to Living Building Projects train the users how to properly use the building, new schools need to educate their staff on proper protocol and how these new procedures support the school and the students.

Overall the feedback received illuminated a disconnect between why the building is designed a certain way and how the users understand how to use it. By educating from the ground up about how the environment influences the students, teachers and staff, problems with usability should decrease. If the occupants understand the benefits and support the change, resistance should decrease with time. The members of the workshop support the Toolkit© as a third party educational tool that supports the designers and users to level the conversation and enhance the design and usability of school design.

PLANNING + PROGRAMMING
EXPLORE

ARCHITECTURAL STRATEGIES

CAMPUS + BUILDING SECURITY

OPEN SPACE

LANDSCAPING - GREEN SPACE

DAYLIGHTING

INDOOR/OUTDOOR ENVIRONMENTS

SPACES FOR EXERCISE

VARIED SIZES OF SPACES

INFORMAL LEARNING SPACES

FLEXIBILITY

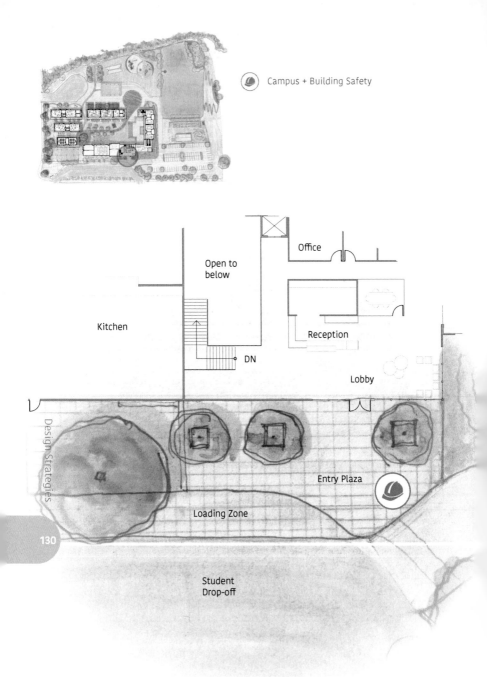

Campus + Building Safety

Open to below

Office

Kitchen

Reception

DN

Lobby

Entry Plaza

Loading Zone

Student Drop-off

Figure 4.1 Proposed controlled Single Entrance, Monte Vista Elementary, Vista, CA

CAMPUS + BUILDING SECURITY

The safety section in chapter 2 under the Nine Principles of Learning Environments for Creativity, shows that safety in schools is a complex issue. Safety in schools is not easily solved by architecture **alone**. Architecture and physical environments do have an impact on human behavior, perceived safety and ability to adapt to a given situation or threat. However the trend of hardening schools, building taller fences, and creating spaces that are "hyper secure" will not solve the safety problem the schools in the United States face. Hardening of schools can even have the opposite effect, creating an environment that is not welcoming and propagates an continuous underlying unease in the occupants of the space, causing them to behave as though there is a threat in their space, even when there isn't.

With this in mind, the architecture of a school does have a substantial impact on how safe it feels and include safety features to react in various situations. Common practice now includes a single point of entry and technology in place to monitor traffic in and out of the school. The school should always remain welcoming, even while restricted to outsiders.

If a perimeter fence is required in the schools jurisdiction strive for a design that is visually softer than traditional vertical bars and chain link, reminiscent of detention facilities. Perception of safety within the secured school is extremely important.

RESOURCES

Educational Service District 112 CSG (2019). **Safety and Security for our Futures: a framework for developing a more secure k-12 built environment in Washington** (white paper). https://www.k12construction.org/wp-content/uploads/2019/10/CSG-ESD-White-Paper-2019.pdf

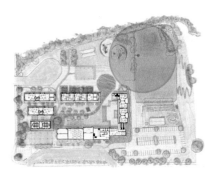

(🏃) Spaces for Exercise

(🌲) Landscaping + Green Space

(🌄) Open Space

(🧍) Informal Learning Spaces

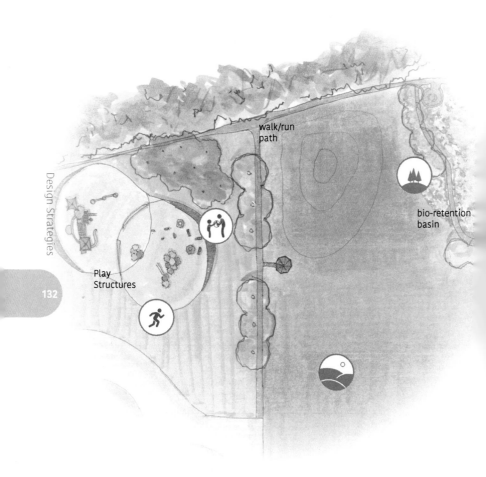

walk/run
path

bio-retention
basin

Play
Structures

Figure 4.2 Proposed
playgrounds and open field,
Monte Vista Elementary, Vista, CA

OPEN SPACE

Exposure to and physical interaction with natural environments as well as activities in natural settings replenish the attentional system located in the prefrontal cortex of the brain. Such exposure to nature can help improve concentration needed to learn and perform tasks such as reading or writing. The impacts of exposure to nature on higher level cognitive functions, including creativity, have not yet been explored in depth. However, the research does suggest that because of the restorative affect on the attention span and exposure to varied stimuli, integrating natural environments for informal learning and physical activity in a school setting would help promote creative thinking.

Open spaces on a school campus serve as a benefit to the campus in numerous ways. It allows for large outdoor gathers, informal learning space, and room to run and play for the students. This supports the students socializing opportunities, learning environment variation, exposure to nature, and exercise needs.

If the open space is grass/turf it also contributes to the overall green and natural landscape of the school, which has been proven to support health and wellbeing. Adding variation to the types of landscaping on campus supports the need for varied stimuli discussed in chapter 2.

RESOURCES

Gilavand, A., Espidkar, F., & Gilavand, M. (2016). **Investigating the Impact of Schools' Open Space on Learning and Educational Achievement of Elementary Students.** International Journal of Pediatrics, 4(4), 1663- 1670.

LANDSCAPING + GREEN SPACE

"Scientific inquiry has demonstrated the positive effects of green spaces on physical health, mental well-being, social connectivity, and human behaviors. It is now believed that we can take these concepts and apply them to education. The design of today's school buildings and spaces is beginning to reflect the values of green and healthy learning environments as communities are being incorporated more green spaces in educational facility planning and design." (Ozer, 2007).

As mentioned in chapter two, direct access to natural environments has a positive impact on learning, attention, and creativity. Even in urban settings, landscaping and green spaces provide restorative qualities. Landscaping shapes the way the site is used, carving out spaces of varying sizes and sensorial stimuli, ideal for creative learning environments.

RESOURCES

Atchley RA, Strayer DL, Atchley P (2012) **Creativity in the Wild: Improving Creative Reasoning through Immersion in Natural Settings**. PLoS ONE 7(12):e51474.

SPACES FOR EXERCISE

Providing adequate indoor and outdoor space for physical movement is essential. Research shows the physical exercise positively impacts nearly every aspect of human health. Including hormone regulation, anxiety and depression regulation, in addition to building strength, and in the case of children, letting out excess energy. In a learning environment, physical activity also allows the mind to take a break, and digest any information learned during class. This is important for memory formation and retention.

The architectural solutions include both interior open spaces, and outdoor spaces. Depending on your climate and surrounding context this will vary. These settings should follow the same principles of the other educational settings, providing adequate daylight, ventilation and air quality, acoustics and varied stimuli. Air quality, thermal comfort and acoustics are particularly important in these environments considering the high volume and high physical activity of the users.

RESOURCES

Strong, W. B., Malina, R. M., Blimkie, C. J. R., Daniels, S. R., Dishman, R. K., Gutin, B., ... Trudeau, F. (2005). **Evidence Based Physical Activity for School-age Youth**. The Journal of Pediatrics, 146(6), 732–737. https://doi.org/10.1016/j.jpeds.2005.01.055

 Spaces for Exercise

 Landscaping + Green Space

 Daylighting

 Indoor/Outdoor Environments

Figure 4.3 (Below) Proposed classroom building renovation section, Monte Vista Elementary, Vista, CA

Figure 4.4 (Right) landscaped bioretention basin to double as outdoor learning environment.

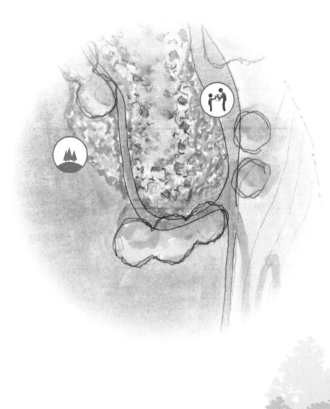

DAYLIGHT

Many existing schools do not have adequate daylight in the classrooms. If a modernization allows it, increasing the amount of daylight entering a room will dramatically improve the classroom atmosphere and make it easier to visually process information. Caution must be taken, depending on the climate of the project, to provide adequate shading and appropriate openings depending on the sun angle, heat gain potential and glare risk.

Maximizing indirect daylight warranted the greatest improvement. Direct sunlight during parts of the day were found to create glare and discomfort. The quality of electrical lighting makes a significant impact. Classrooms with high quality and good distribution of light saw the most student progress. Modern approaches to increased interior daylighting include solar-tubes, or automated shade systems controlled via programmed software or sensors.

RESOURCES

Barrett, P., Davies, F., Zhang, Y., & Barrett, L. (2015). **The impact of classroom design on pupils' learning: Final results of a holistic, multi-level analysis. Building and Environment**, 89, 118-133.

Heschong, L., Wright, R, Okura, S. (1999). **Daylighting and productivity: elementary school studies.** Consumer Behavior and Non-Energy Effects, 8(149).

INDOOR/OUTDOOR
ENVIRONMENTS

As curriculum shifts from analytical teaching to interactive, project based learning, more space is required for assignments and activities. Environments which blend indoor and outdoor environments lend themselves to increased utilization due to the flexible nature of these spaces. These blended environments increase student interest and attention. Natural environments restore students and teachers attention. These environments tend to be informal which encourages students to play and explore ideas outside of the rigidity of conventional assignments.

Where climate and site permits, including outdoor spaces directly adjacent to classrooms allows for the learning space to extend beyond the walls of the classroom. Teachers can use this space and needed, granting students use of this space for small group break out areas, while remaining visually supervised.

Other schools may not have the opportunity to have outdoor spaces as a direct extension of the classroom but can utilize outdoor learning spaces throughout campus or designated rooms that do connect to the outdoors, taking their entire class there for activities. Climate must always be considered when designing an outdoor learning environment that can be used throughout the year.

Daylighting

Indoor/Outdoor Environments

Informal Learning Spaces

Varied Spaces

Figure 4.5 (Above) Existing typical classroom

Figure 4.6 Proposed Play loft, Monte Vista Elementary, Vista, CA

VARIED SPACES

Alternating stimuli is key in developing creativity. It promotes exploration, supplying zones which are more ideal for various types of learners and activities. Especially for children in lower grades, spaces must to be designed appropriately for their scale - that means smaller spaces, even spaces which are not comfortable for adults to inhabit.

Learning is reliant on neuroplasticity; the ability of neurons to change and reorganize based on experiences and the environment. At the Academy of Neuroscience for Architecture (ANFA) Conference in 2016, Margaret Tarampi addressed how enriched environments impact neuroplasticity. This concept is important for creative thinking because it is at the foundation of absorbing and processing new information. Studies show that enriched environments; meaning enriched for visual, motor, cognitive and somatosensory that the environment foster neuroplasticity and learning. The built environment can either foster or detrimentally harm this neural plasticity.

Healthy social engagement also plays a roll in learning, and neuroplasticity and the physical environment promotes different types of social interactions.

"Making a learning environment truly inclusive means designing from multiple developmental perspectives"

-The Third Teacher

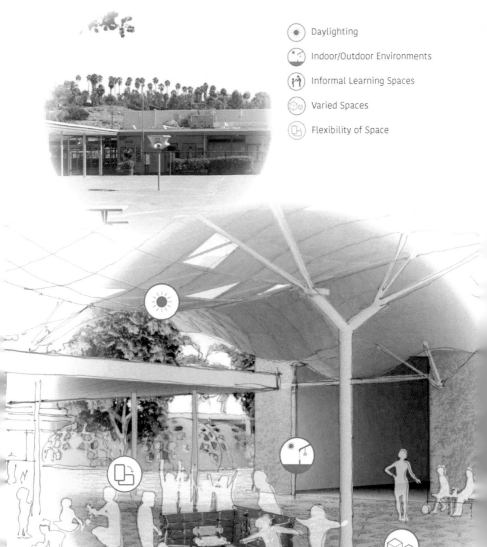

Daylighting

Indoor/Outdoor Environments

Informal Learning Spaces

Varied Spaces

Flexibility of Space

Figure 4.7 (Above) existing kindergarten play area

Figure 4.8 Proposed Makers Court, Monte Vista ES.

INFORMAL LEARNING SPACES

Creating spaces outside of the classroom to host various activities increased student engagement and willingness to learn. The brain prioritizes novel information which can be done through Introducing information in unusual ways or different environments. These spaces are not prescriptive. Some options include a "makers space," gardens, and break out spaces within the school and outdoors as the site and climate allows.

These spaces are sometimes misunderstood as redundant spaces beyond the typical classroom requirement. However, informal spaces allow for increased flexibility in curriculum and teaching approached. Catering to the myriad of learning styles and encouraging student ownership and engagement. Informal settings can occur anywhere, including outside, or existing circulation. While it can increase the required space for learning, the benefits of increased student interest are considerable.

Design Strategies

143

RESOURCES

Davies, D., Jindal-Snape, D., Collier, C., Digby, R., Hay, P., & Howe, A. (2013). **Creative learning environments in education—A systematic literature review.** Thinking Skills and Creativity, 8, 80-91.

○ Daylighting

▲ Landscaping + Green Space

⚇ Informal Learning Spaces

⬡ Varied Spaces

14

Figure 4.9 Central Courtyard,
Monte Vista ES

Figure 4.10 Existing informal spaces to remain, Monte Vista ES

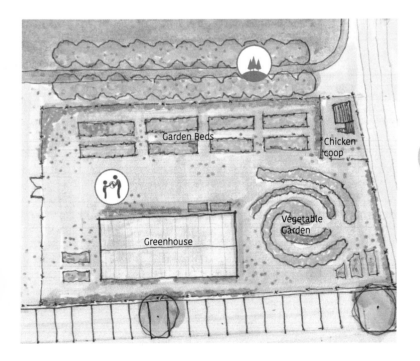

Garden Beds

Chicken coop

Greenhouse

Vegetable Garden

Figure 4.11 Proposed garden, Monte Vista ES

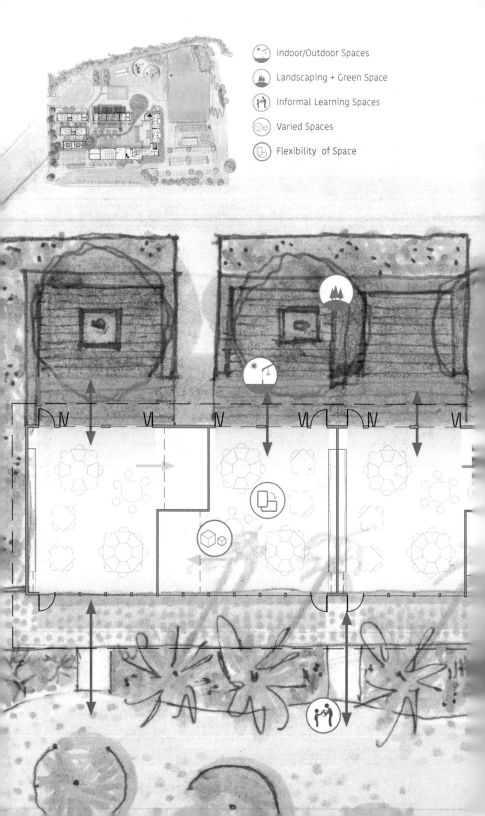

Indoor/Outdoor Spaces

Landscaping + Green Space

Informal Learning Spaces

Varied Spaces

Flexibility of Space

FLEXIBILITY OF SPACE

Adaptability and flexibility are key attributes of any facility to withstand the change of pedagogy and use over the lifetime of the school. Adaptive architecture allows for the spaces to change over time through small interventions or larger renovations. This could mean the school is designed to be expanded overtime and blend together with the main campus. It could mean spaces are designed to allow for rooms to be combined to divided with minimal structural or plumbing modifications.

Flexibility allows for daily changes and promotes ownership and autonomy of the space. Flexibility includes furniture (see furniture, fixtures and equipment in this chapter for more), as well as architectural elements such as operable partitions and large enough spaces to establish smaller zones of learning, controlled by the teacher and students.

This will look different at each age, as students develop and respond to environmental stimuli and pedagogy and curriculum changes. Classrooms supporting younger students who primarily inhabit a single classroom for the entire day will look different than a high school learning environment where students have more independence and require less direct supervision and move from room to room during the course of a day. Creating beautiful, fun spaces for all ages will inspire both children and teachers to promote involvement and increase enthusiasm.

Figure 4.12 Proposed modified Classrooms to include direct access to the outdoors, MVES

SCHEMATIC DESIGN | DEVELOP

ARCHITECTURAL STRATEGIES

AIR QUALITY - NATURAL + MECHANICAL

THERMAL COMFORT

TECHNOLOGY - TEACHING TOOLS

TECHNOLOGY - BUILDING SYSTEMS

AIR QUALITY - NATURAL + MECHANICAL

Many of the existing school facilities occupied today in the United States have unacceptable indoor conditions. Poor air quality, high levels of Carbon Dioxide (CO_2) can lead to children getting sick, or worsening asthma symptoms, resulting in the child staying home from school. As previously mentioned in England (Barrett, Davies, Zhang, & Barrett, 2015) a holistic study showed student performance improved with increased natural ventilation or mechanical systems with higher air exchange rates, reducing the CO2 levels in the classroom.

The outdated existing facilities have seriously compromised air quality, with obsolete mechanical systems, and toxic finishes. The air exchange and ventilation system must be evaluated and updated in these facilities. Breathing fresh air promotes health and improves alertness and attention.

RESOURCES

ASHRAE 2018. **Advanced Energy Design Guide for K-12 School Building: Achieving Zero Energy** https://www.ashrae.org/technical-resources/aedgs/zero-energy-aedg-free-download

Barrett, P., Davies, F., Zhang, Y., & Barrett, L. (2015). **The impact of classroom design on pupils' learning: Final results of a holistic, multi-level analysis.** Building and Environment, 89, 118-133.

THERMAL COMFORT

In addition to insuring sufficient ventilation and air exchange, the building envelope must be designed for thermal comfort. Thermal comfort is vital component in how students perform. Thermal stress in a classroom, either hot or cold, will significantly depress performance and attention of the students (Mishra, 2015). The discomfort caused by thermal in-balance also decreased engagement. Similar to indoor air quality, thermal comfort directly impacts student and teacher health as ability to function within the space. When the perceived thermal comfort in either temperature or humidity extreme, higher cognitive functions including creativity are impossible. The ideal thermal comfort zone depends on the schools region and subsequent climate and cultural expectations.

Design Strategies

151

RESOURCES

ASHRAE 2018. **Advanced Energy Design Guide for K-12 School Building: Achieving Zero Energy** https://www.ashrae.org/technical-resources/aedgs/ zero-energy-aedg-free-download

Mishra, A.K., Ramgopal, M. (2015). **A comparison of student performance between conditioned and naturally ventilated classrooms.** Building and Environments, 84, 181-188

TECHNOLOGY –
TEACHING TOOLS

The use of technology in learning environments is in constant flux. The built environment must accommodate this constant change and still provide ideal space if this technology is not available. In Lifelong Kindergarten, Resnick (2017) states "too often, designers of educational materials and activities simply add a thin layer of technology and gaming over antiquated curriculum and pedagogy, somewhat like putting lipstick on a pig." This same concept translates to how, in some cases, technology is applied to learning environments. The teaching tools in the classroom are dependent on the curriculum approach. Technology is a powerful tool when it comes to learning and architecture, however a poorly designed space with state of the art technology will ultimately fail the students.

RESOURCES

Resnick, M., & Robinson, K. (2017). **Lifelong kindergarten: cultivating creativity through projects, passion, peers, and play.** Cambridge, MA: The MIT Press.

Brock, L. L., Nishida, T. K., Chiong, C., Grimm, K. J., & Rimm-Kaufman, S. E. (2008). **Children's perceptions of the classroom environment and social and academic performance: A longitudinal analysis of the contribution of the Responsive Classroom approach.** Journal of School Psychology, 2, 129-149.

TECHNOLOGY - BUILDING SYSTEMS

Building systems and technology have developed a step beyond many of the strategies discussed previously. For example heating and cooling, lighting, even teaching technology can be automated and advanced. These systems can operate without high tech building systems and sensors. Recent and developing projects are implementing smart systems that control different elements within the building including heating and cooling systems, daylight and occupancy sensors, fire alarm and lock-down systems, and wireless technology for mobile blended learning systems, etc. Building technologies should be reviewed for appropriateness of long range goals, immediate scope and budget of the project. Influence on creativity of students is uncertain at this time and will evolve with further research in the future.

RESOURCES

ASHRAE 2018. **Advanced Energy Design Guide for K-12 School Building: Achieving Zero Energy** https://www.ashrae.org/technical-resources/aedgs/ zero-energy-aedg-free-download

Open Space

Landscaping + Green Space

Indoor/Outdoor Spaces

Varied Spaces

Spaces for Exercise

Safety

Informal Learning Spaces

Daylight

Figure 4.13 (Left) existing unused space between classroom building and portables.

Figure 4.14 (Below) Proposed central courtyard, MVES, Vista, CA

NOTES

DESIGN DEVELOPMENT | REFINE

ARCHITECTURAL STRATEGIES

FURNITURE, FIXTURE + EQUIPMENT

ELECTRICAL LIGHTING

ACOUSTICS

MATERIALITY

Figure 4.15 Furniture intervention, Orange County High School Classroom Pilot Project, HED (ANFA, 2016)

FIXTURE, FURNITURE + EQUIPMENT

A study performed by Harley Ellis Devereaux (HED) four High Schools in Orange County School District, California, demonstrated the significance of furniture in the classroom. The experiment aimed to create highly flexible environments that radically changed the configuration of a standard existing classroom. The high schools involved in this experiment were untouched since they were built 30 years ago, with furniture from the same era. However these schools, like many across the country, don't have the means to do extensive renovations yet, but need to improve the classroom environment and student engagement (ANFA Conference, 2016.)

Changing the furniture out from outdated, heavy desks and chairs to mobile, versatile furniture allows the teacher to facilitate multiple activities at once and accommodate several learning styles. The classrooms can be transform from a large group to small group settings based on their individual needs, giving the ownership of the space to the users. Students reported feeling more engaged, and excited to learn and participate in class. Some users even described the spaces as "brighter" despite only the furniture changing. The students perception of the space changed and inspired them.

RESOURCES

Breithecker, D. (2009). **Bodies in motion, brains in motion.** Federal Institute on the Development of Posture and Exercise. https://www.aquestdesign.ca/docs/45-066-02_V01_EN_Bodies_in_Motion-120602.pdf

Teacher desks can be more mobile. This could include fixed or mobile storage, an adjustable height media desk, or a traditional teacher desk.

Soft floor seating is good for break out spaces, reading areas, or other projects. Younger kids in particular like working on the floor. Washable mats make the area comfortable while still easy to clean.

Raised soft seating is also a good option. These types of benches can come upholstered in a vinyl-like fabric, soft to the touch and easy to wipe down and keep clean.

Figure 4.16 Flexible furniture examples (VSAmerica, 2020)

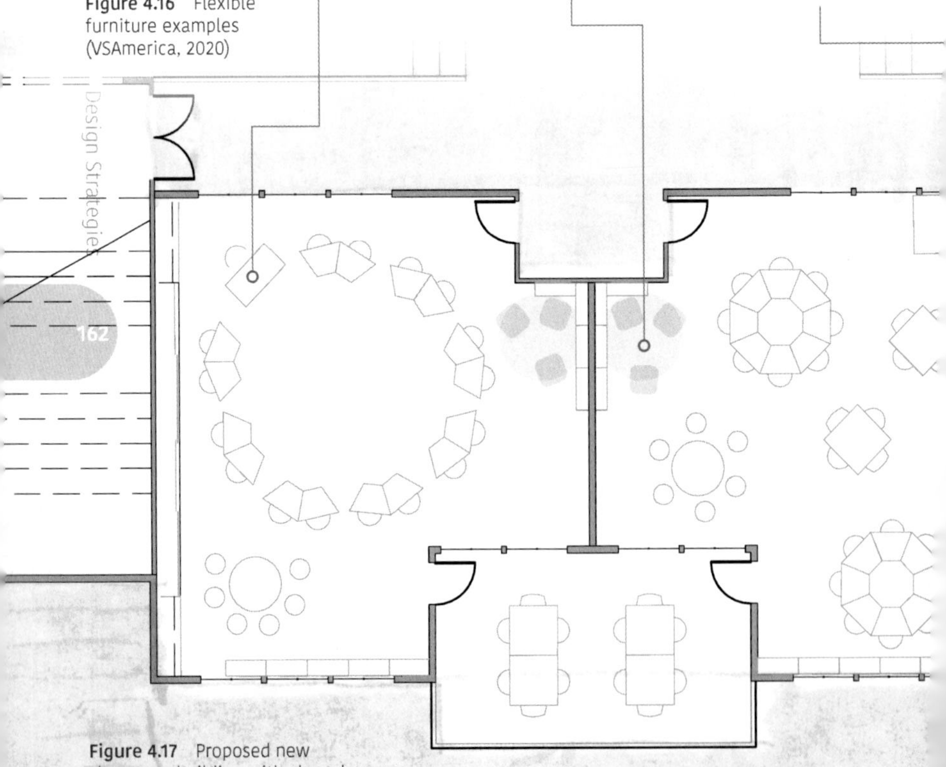

Figure 4.17 Proposed new classroom building with shared outdoor enclosed breakout spaces.

In addition to the fixed storage in the classroom, short, mobile shelving and cubbies are good for flexibility. These should be easy enough to move by the teacher when setting up their space and sturdy enough a child cannot cause it to tip over. All rolling casework should have locking casters.

A variety of student work spaces should be provided. For additional flexibility consider folding or stacking tables to move out of the way depending on the class arrangement. Tables should be easily moved by students and have locking casters.

Student chairs should be easy to move by students. There are options that allow for comfortable fidgeting, and movement as well as different seating positions for all students.

ELECTRIC LIGHTING

Lighting has a significant impact on how the brain functions and the bodies circadian rhythms. The lighting in a space influences the ease of difficulty to read, see across the room, or the task on the desk. Cooler light temperatures can cause headaches or make it difficult to view certain levels of information and data. The brain regulates hormones based on lighting and circadian cycles. As the sunlight changes throughout the day, the body changes.

According to Barrett, Davies, Zhang (2015), "Not only the quality but also the quantity of electrical lighting has a significant positive correlation with the pupil's learning progress. This studies found that students performed best under full-spectrum fluorescent lamps with ultraviolet supplements compared to students in other lighting conditions. Daylight provides the broadest spectrum of light and is ideal to use as much as possible. High quality electrical lighting can supplement and provide lighting as needed during the day or year when daylight is limited.

RESOURCES

Barrett, P., Davies, F., Zhang, Y., & Barrett, L. (2015). **The impact of classroom design on pupils' learning: Final results of a holistic, multi-level analysis.** Building and Environment, 89, 118-133.

Heschong, L., Wright, R, Okura, S. (1999). **Daylighting and productivity: elementary school studies.** Consumer Behavior and Non-Energy Effects, 8(149).

ACOUSTICS

Acoustics are a fundamental requirement for learning and creativity. A classroom, or other learning environments require acoustic conditions for instruction, quiet individual work, and large group work which may be a higher volume. If the room does not adequately manage this range in volumes and tasks the student will either be unable to properly hear the teacher, or the room may be too noisy to focus on a task at hand. A room with poor acoustics can prevent students from hearing the teacher when needed or, on the other hand, not dampen excessive noise pollution and create an environment too loud for certain tasks or concentration.

Acoustic treatments are relatively easy to add and adjust in exciting facilities with surface treatments for disbursement and dampening of sound. If the facility construction is inadequate and sounds travel from one part of the building to another, this becomes more challenging to retrofit, but still possible.

New facilities and larger modification projects have the opportunity to create more ideal acoustical atmospheres in both the classrooms and other spaces throughout the school. Implementing acoustical strategies from non-parallel wall configurations to acoustical treatments is possible at this scale and will improve the comfort and usability of the space.

Acoustics

Fixture, Furniture + Equipment

Indoor/Outdoor Spaces

Informal Learning Spaces

Flexible Spaces

Daylight

Materiality

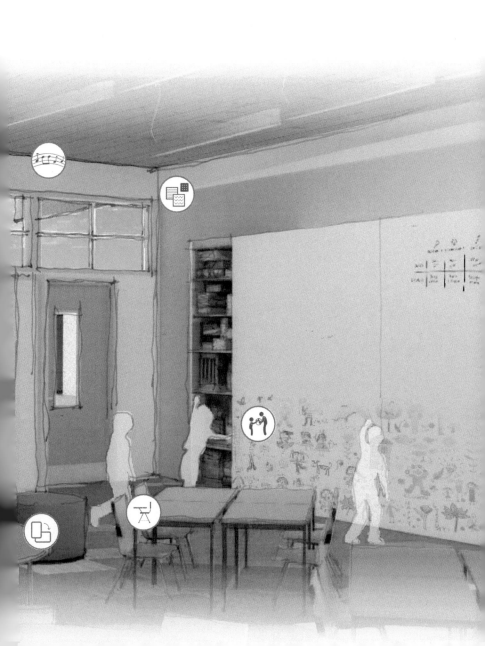

Figure 4.18 (Left) Existing typical classroom

Figure 4.19 (Below) proposed open classroom with connections to outdoor learning spaces.

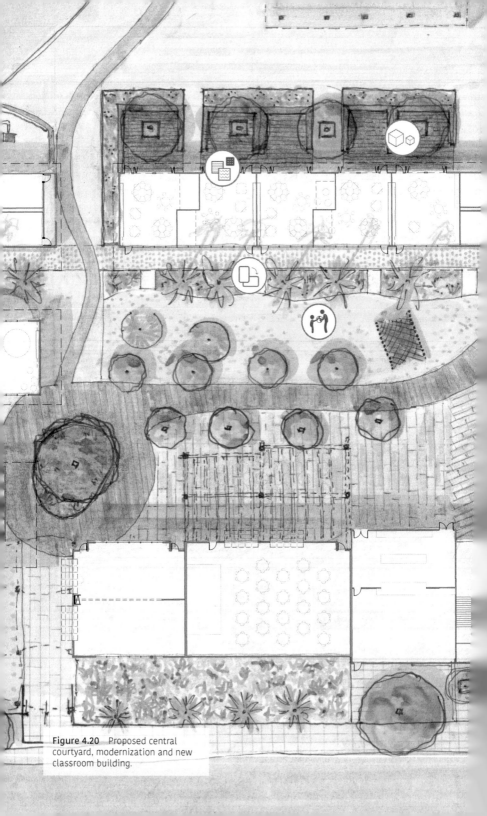

Figure 4.20 Proposed central courtyard, modernization and new classroom building.

MATERIALITY

The quality of the learning environment directly influences the level of enthusiasm the users feel. A beautifully designed space that is centered around how people use the space will elevate performance, excitement and respect for the space. Creating a comfortable space is critical to promote students' willingness and eagerness to learn, which directly impacts their ability to think creatively. Materiality preferences and appropriateness depends on the location of the building and the culture of the community. However some colors have the same impact across the board.

Materiality of the site and the classroom influences a multitude of qualities including: acoustics, lighting, visual stimuli, auditory stimuli, and usability of surfaces. Materials used in schools require a high level of durability and ease of maintenance. As technology advancements are made, maintenance changes and requires training staff on new procedures to sustain longevity of materials.

Natural and low VOC (volatile organic compound) materials are encouraged and promote health and well-being of the building inhabitants as well as global sustainability efforts. These materials will be different depending on the region of the project and availability of building materials and finishes.

RESOURCES

Volatile Organic Compounds' Impact on Indoor Air Quality. (2017, November 06). Retrieved from https://www.epa.gov/indoor-air-quality-iaq/volatile-organic-compounds-impact-indoor-air-quality

Design Strategies

CASE STUDY DESIGN:
VISTA UNIFIED SCHOOL DISTRICT
MISSION + GOALS

MISSION

The Mission of Vista Unified School District is to inspire each and every student to persevere as critical thinking individuals who collaborate to solve real world problems.

VISION

Our Vision in Vista Unified School District (VUSD) is to be the model of education excellence and innovation.

VALUES

Our Values is show Respect by treating all with dignity. Trust by having confidence that every decision focuses on the best interests of students. By collaboration, working in a collective partnership with clear two-way dialogue that builds relationships among home, school, and the community.

*per Vista Unified School District Long Range Facilities Master Plan 2016

Formerly a canyon, this site was filled in when the school was designed and constructed in 1964 and remains at that grade to this date. The property to the north is undeveloped and protected natural environment that acts as a natural barrier to the school site. To the east is a large hill, scaling 40 feet above the school site at the high point. This lot is vacant except for a few small homes at the north end of the property. To the west and the south are the main roads, both of which access the MVES.

MONTE VISTA ELEMENTARY
SCHOOL PROPOSAL

The site of Monte Vista Elementary School (MVES) is located on a flat site that is depressed approximately six feet below the primary road and drop off to the south of the site. This proposal developed contrast and size between different outdoor spaces to create hierarchy across the site. The original permanent structures receive modernization, blending indoor and outdoor learning environments. The relocatable buildings on site are demolished and replaced with a new, two-story building. The new building features the multi-purpose room, library, and replacement classrooms. The architectural form of the building provides a secure campus environment. Removing the semipermanent structures in the center of campus allows for a newly activated central courtyard. This courtyard becomes an enriched learning environment, blending classes and providing a setting for experiments and play to occur. Quieter, small scale natural environments hug the perimeter of the structures. These spaces are intended as semi-private extensions of their adjacent spaces.

On the outer edges of the site more 'natural' environments occur, including the water retention/bioswale which doubles as a teaching station, a hiking trail to the top of the sites 40 foot hill on the east side. To the north end of the site are the designated play structures. The student gardens are located at the south east portion of the site, next to the parking lot for community access during off hours and weekends.

Figure 4.21 Proposed site plan for
Monte Vista Elementary School.

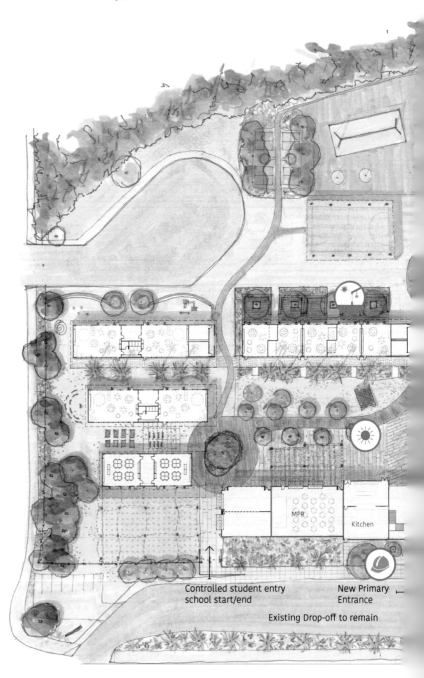

MPR

Kitchen

Controlled student entry
school start/end

New Primary
Entrance

Existing Drop-off to remain

Solar Array
Canopy

Repave, re-stripe
existing parking lot

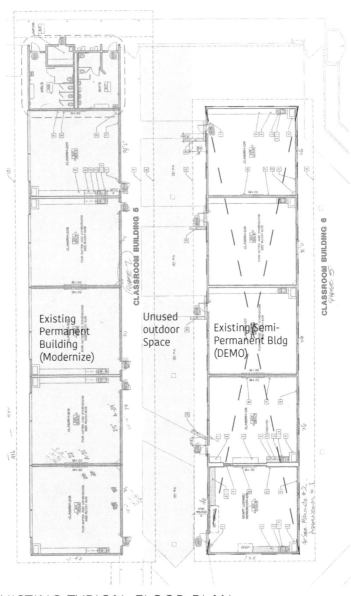

Existing
Permanent
Building
(Modernize)

Unused
outdoor
Space

Existing Semi-
Permanent Bldg
(DEMO)

CLASSROOM BUILDING 5

CLASSROOM BUILDING 6

EXISTING TYPICAL FLOOR PLAN

10'   20'

Figure 4.22 Existing and proposed
floor plans. MVES

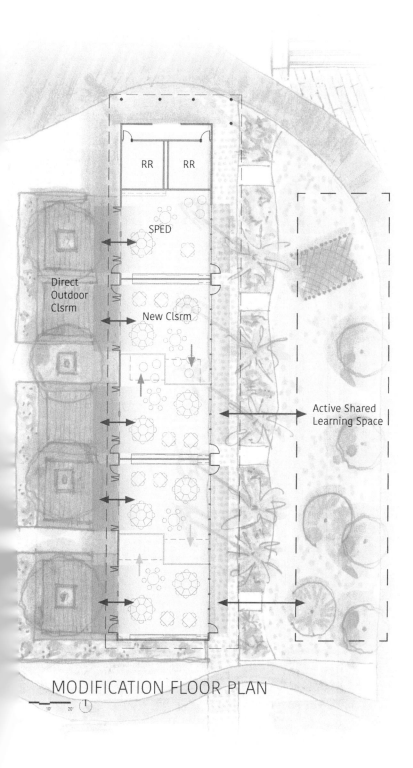

RR RR

SPED

Direct
Outdoor
Clsrm

New Clsrm

Active Shared
Learning Space

MODIFICATION FLOOR PLAN

10'   20'

5

CONCLUSION

The public education system in the United States, and the world, is experiencing a shift. 21st Century education emphasizes creativity, innovation, collaboration, self-driven, and personalized learning. Students today are being prepared for jobs that are unknown. This requires a high level of flexibility and adaptability in curriculum and learning opportunities. This is where the architecture of schools is falling short.

This changing curriculum and approach is being taught in facilities that are outdated, and under performing. Classrooms often have minimal daylight, inadequate heating and cooling systems, limited to nonexistent usable outdoor learning environments, classrooms with heavy or built in furniture that do not promote flexibility or ownership. All of this is physically and mentally detrimental to both the teachers and students occupying the space. Many of the schools in operation today were built in the mid 1900's have seen minimal modernizations to date outside of basic access compliance. Updating or replacing these facilities is the ideal, however impossible due to the school funding infrastructure.

The school districts with the facilities in the worst conditions, struggle the most to pass bonds and fund these improvement projects or new schools. Even the districts with the money to repair and replace schools need a guideline for design that supports the physical and mental needs of the users, based on science, that allow for adaptability and flexibility for the curriculum of tomorrow. This project uncovers that evidence. It explores the cognitive behaviors of creative minds, the level of stimuli needed for learning and engagement, the environmental minimums acceptable for 21st century learning. It prioritizes needs, so that a given school and a given budget has a target.

In an effort to make this information accessible to those who need it - teachers, school administration, architects, state agencies, etc - the development of a Toolkit document became evident. The Learning Environments for Creativity Toolkit is an educational tool to shed light on what works and doesn't work in school facility design, as well as a foundational understanding of why creativity is the goal, how it works, and what influences it in developing brains. It will continue to grow and change as research continues, with future editions, and updates on the website www.buildingcreativeschools.org.

NEXT STEPS

Collaboration and resilience have shown to be key factors in changing the physical state of schools and stakeholder mind-set throughout this investigatory process. A top down approach to change is ineffective in today's design constraints and opportunities. Engaging all levels and educating everyone involved is the only way change can happen. This education comes from science, but also from experience. Each division of the industry needs to listen to the others, and engage in a conversation that empowers everyone from students to teachers to facilities managers to architects.

Changing facility design does not rest solely on the architect. The architect must strive to learn as much about the built and emerging environment as possible, but also about how students, teachers and parents use the space; what works, what doesn't. Equally essential, students, parents and teachers must investigate what elements of their surrounding have considerable impact on them. Nothing will replace a great teacher. A great teacher can teach in the worst environment. But they should never have to. School design historically has been led by intuition, now it can be led by evidence.

Listen to the students, to the parents, and to the teachers. If someone asks for something, or complains about something, listen to why they are dissatisfied, and aim to understand their perspective. Go beyond the basic needs of learning environments, and engage those impacted by the space. Changes in this system are possible when communication is effective and equal, when everyone's voice is heard, and robust evidence based information is circulated, discussed and developed.

GET INVOLVED | GIVE FEEDBACK

Collaboration is vital for success of future school designs. That includes your voice, your perspective. Schools impact all of us and everyone can have an impact. In order to keep this project evolving, your input is needed. If you see want more information on a topic, find something is particularly helpful, have a new resource to add, we want to hear from you.

Please come join the conversation at:

BuildingCreativeSchools.org and
Instagram @bldgcreativeschools

REFERENCES

ANFA 2016: "How Educational Environments Impact Learning" -Dale, Gallagher, Tarampi, Zandvliet – ANFA | Academy of Neuroscience for Architecture. (n.d.). Retrieved January 29, 2018, from http://anfarch.org/anfa2016_daleetal/

ANFA 2014: "Neuroscience and Design for Special Needs – Learning Environments" -Dale, Gallagher, Tarampi, Zandvliet – ANFA | Academy of Neuroscience for Architecture. (n.d.). Retrieved January 29, 2018, from https://www.youtube.com/watch?v=t6ThdFtKzil

Architects, V. (2017). Verstas Architects. Retrieved from http://verstasarkkitehdit.fi/projects/saunalahti-school

Atchley RA, Strayer DL, Atchley P (2012) Creativity in the Wild: Improving Creative Reasoning through Immersion in Natural Settings. PLoS ONE 7(12):e51474.

Barrett, P., Davies, F., Zhang, Y., & Barrett, L. (2015). The impact of classroom design on pupils' learning: Final results of a holistic, multi-level analysis. Building and Environment, 89, 118-133.

Bateson, P., & Martin, P. (2013). Play, playfulness, creativity and innovation. Cambridge: Cambridge University Press.

Bowen, Ryan S., (2017). Understanding by Design. Vanderbilt University Center for Teaching. Retrieved [January 2018] from https://cft.vanderbilt.edu/understanding-by-design/.

Brand, S., Vossen, P. (2014). How to Inspire the Next Generation of Creative Thinkers and Innovators. The Creative Post. Retrieved February 13, 2018, from http://www.creativitypost.com

Brock, L. L., Nishida, T. K., Chiong, C., Grimm, K. J., &

Rimm-Kaufman, S. E. (2008). Children's perceptions of the classroom environment and social and academic performance: A longitudinal analysis of the contribution of the Responsive Classroom approach. Elsevier, 129-149.

Cannon Design, VS Furniture, & Bruce Mau Design. (2010). The Third Teacher. New York: Abrams.

Chesnokova, O., Subbatsky, E. (2014). Social creativity in primary-school children: how to measure, develop and accept it. Procedia - Social and Behavior Sciences, 146, 141-146.

Craft, A. (2001). An analysis of research and literature on Creativity in Education. Qualifications and Curriculum Authority.

Corpley, A. J. (1995). Fostering creativity in the classroom: General principles. In M. Runco (Ed.), The creativity research handbook Vol. 1 (P..83-114). Cresskill, NJ: Hampton Press.

Daily, A. (2013, July). Arch Daily. Retrieved from http://www.archdaily.com/406513/saunalahti-school-verstas-architects

Dictionary. (2018). creativity. (n.d.). Dictionary.com Unabridged. Retrieved March 23, 2018 from http://www.dictionary.com

Dietrich, Arne. (2004) The Cognitive Neuroscience of Creativity. Psychonomic Bulletin & Review 11.6: 1011-026.

Dobkins, K. (2016). Using Neuroscience to tailor visual environments for infants and children. San Diego, CA.

Duarte, R., Gomes, M.G, Rodrigues, A.M.(2017) Classroom ventilation with manual opening of windows: findings from a two-year-long experimental study of a Portuguese secondary school. Building and Environment, 124, 118-129.

Eberhard, J. P. (2009). Brain Landscape: the coexistance of neuroscience and architecture. Oxford: Oxford University Press.

Educational Service District 112 CSG (2019). Safety and Security for our Futures: a framework for developing a more secure k-12 built environment in Washington (white paper). https://www.k12construction.org/wp-content/uploads/2019/10/CSG-ESD-White-Paper-2019.pdf

Esquivel, G.B. (1995). Teacher behaviors that foster creativity. Educational Psychology Review, 7(2), 185-202.

Fasko, Jr., D. (2001). Education and Creativity. (I. Lawrence Erlbaum Associates, Ed.) Creativity Research Journal, 13, 317-327.

Filardo, M., & Vincent, J. M. (2017). Adequate & Equitable US PK-12 Infrastructure: Priority Actions for Systemic Reform. A Report from the Planning for PK-12 School Infrastructure National Initiative. 21st Century School Fund.

Gaier, E., Dellas, M. (1971). Concept formation and creativity in children. Theory into Practice, 10.2, 117-123.

Gilavand, A., Espidkar, F., & Gilavand, M. (2016). Investigating the Impact of Schools' Open Space on Learning and Educational Achievement of Elementary Students. International Journal of Pediatrics, 4(4), 1663- 1670.

Guilford, J.P. (2017). Can creativity by developed? Art Education 11.6, 3-7, 14-18.

Gotbaum, R. (Writer). (2017, October 14). When The Focus Is On The Student, Not The Class [Radio broadcast]. In Weekend Edition Saturday. NPR.

Hancock, L. (2011, September). Why Are Finland's Schools Successful? Smithsonianmag.com. Retrieved from https://www.smithsonianmag.com/innovation/why-are-finlands-schools-successful-49859555/

Hashim, A. K., Strunk, K. O., & Marsh, J. A. (2018). The new school advantage. Examining the effects of strategic new school openings on student achievement. Economics of Education Review, 62, 254-266.

Humlum, M. K., & Smith, N. (2015). Long-term effects of school size on students' outcomes. Economics of Education Review, 45, 28-43.

Hosey, L. (2017). Redesigning Innovation. Newschool of Architecture + Design San Diego, CA.

Iversn, A., Godina-Martinez, G., Hankard, N., Buehring, A. (2019). "Safe Environments: Reconnecting the Cortext to the classroom", CASH Annual Conference.

Jetsonen, S., Johansson, E., Nuikkinen, K., & Sahlberg, P. (2011). The Best School in the World. Helsinki, Finland: Museum of Finnish Architecture.

Kangas, M. (2010). Finnish children's views on the ideal school and learning environment. Learning Environments Research, 13(3), 205-223.

Kweon, B.S., Ellis, C., Lee, J., Jacobs, K. (2017). The link between school environments and student academic performance. Urban Forestry & Greening, 23, 35-43.

Lippman, P. C. (2010). Evidence-based design of elementary and secondary schools. Hoboken, NJ: J. Wiley.

Malinin L.H. (2016). Creative Practices Embodied, Embedded, and Enacted in Architectural Settings: Toward an Ecological Model of Creativity. Frontiers in Psychology, 6(1978).

Maxwell, L. (2016). School building condition, social climate, student attendance and academic achievement: a mediation model. Journal of Environmental Psychology, 46, 206-216,

McVickar, P.O.L.L.Y. (1959). The Creative Process in Young Children. The Journal of Nursery Education, 14(3), 11-16.

Mellou, E. (1996) Can Creativity be Nurtured in Young Children?, Early Child Development and Care, 119:1, 119-130.

Mishra, A.K., Ramgopal, M. (2015). A comparison of student performance between conditioned and naturally ventilated classrooms. Building and Environments, 84, 181-188

OCED (2011), Designing for Education: Compendium of Exemplary Educational Facilities 2011, OCED Publishing.

Ozer, E.J., 2007. The effects of school gardens on students and schools:conceptualization and considerations for maximizing healthy development. Health Educ. Behav. 34 (6), 846–863.

Poysa, S, et al. (2018). Variation in situation-specific engagement among lower secondary school students. Learning and Instruction, 53, 64-73.

Perkins, L. B., & Bordwell, R. (2010). Building type basics for elementary and secondary schools. Hoboken, NJ: John Wiley & Sons, Inc.

Piffer, D. (2012, April 25). Can creativity be measured? An attempt to clarify the notion of creativity and general directions for future research. Thinking Skills and Creativity(7), 258-264.

PK Yonge DRS. (2012). Kids LOVE new school! [Video]. Retrieved from https://www.youtube.com /watch?v= NT7Sy9APTPo&feature=youtu.be

Rasti, I. (2018, January 11). How Creative Teaching Improves Students' Executive Function Skills. The Creative Post. Retrieved February 13, 2018, from http://www.creativitypost.com

Resnick, M., & Robinson, K. (2017). Lifelong kindergarten: cultivating creativity through projects, passion, peers, and play. Cambridge, MA: The MIT Press.

Rodgers, D.B. (1998) Supporting autonomy in young children. Young Children, 53(3), 75-80.

Russ, S. W. (2014). Pretend Play in Childhood: Foundation of Adult Creativity. Washington: American Psychological Association.

Sarbu, I., Pacurar, C. (2015). Experimental and numerical research to assess indoor environment quality and schoolwork performance in university classrooms. Building and Environments, 93, 141-154.

Schulte, B. (2015, July 06). Do these eight things and you will be more creative and insightful, neuroscientists say. Retrieved April 03, 2018, from https://www.washingtonpost.com/news/inspired-life/wp/2015/07/06/seven-things-to-do-that-neuroscientists-say-will-enhance-insight-and-boost-creativity/?utm_term=.25628cdbb4ba

Senate Ways & Means Committee. (2018, January 29). Public Hearing: Senate Bill 6531 School Construction. Olympia, WA.

Strong, W. B., Malina, R. M., Blimkie, C. J. R., Daniels, S. R., Dishman, R. K., Gutin, B., ... Trudeau, F. (2005). Evidence Based Physical Activity for School-age Youth. The Journal of Pediatrics, 146(6), 732–737. https://doi.org/10.1016/j.jpeds.2005.01.055

Stazi, F., Maspi, F., Ulpiani, G., Perna, C.D. (2017). Indoor air quality and thermal comfort optimization in classrooms developing an automatic system for windows opening and closing. Energy and Buildings, 139, 732-746.

Vandervert, L. R., Schimpf, P. H., & Liu, H. (2007). How working memory and the cerebellum collaborate to produce creativity and innovation. Creativity Research Journal, 19(1), 1-18.

Verstas Architects is responsible for the primary precedence study in this paper. This website provides drawings and design information about the project.

Walker, T. (2017, June 17). BBC Interview: Timothy D. Walker, author of "Teach Like Finland." Retrieved January 29, 2018, from http://taughtbyfinland.com/bbc-world-news-interview/

Withagen R, Caljouw S.R. (2017) Aldo van Eyck's Playgrounds: Aesthetics, Affordances, and Creativity.

Frontiers in Psychology. 8(1130).

World Economic Forum (2016). Finland v the US: one's education system is ranked among the world's best, the other one is the US. (n.d.). Retrieved November 15, 2017, from https://www.weforum.org/agenda/2016/11/finland-has-one-of-the-worlds-best-education-systems-four-ways-it-beats-the-us/

Yildirim, K., Cagatay, K., & Ayalp, N. (2014). Effect of wall colour on the perception of classrooms. Indoor and Built Original Paper Environment , 24, 607-616.

Zumthor, Peter. (2006) A Way of Looking at Things. Thinking Architecture. Birkhauser, Verlag.

About the Author

ABOUT THE AUTHOR

Mackenzie Sims is passionate about learning and designing for creativity and health in an ever-changing education climate. She strives to bridge research, education and design in her work and believes high impact, positive change is possible in a collaborative environment where all voices that are impacted are heard.

She is an Architectural Designer and Project Coordinator, specializing in educational spaces and environments for children that enhance and promote creativity and learning, currently practicing in San Diego, California. During her time in Washington State, she worked on community based projects including master planning with the Tulalip Tribes. Her work has always centered around positive impact on the community.

She holds a Bachelors of Arts in Architectural Studies from the University of Washington, and a Masters of Architecture with a concentration in Neuroscience for Architecture from NewSchool of Architecture and Design. Her work exploring creativity, childhood development, and the built environment, has gained recognition with the American Institute of Architecture (AIA) Los Angeles 2x8 competition, AIA San Diego Student Design of the Year and NewSchool Thesis of the Year in 2018.

Mackenzie is also an enthusiastic volunteer, teaching high school students about Architecture and guest lecturing at NewSchool about design process, research methodologies and graphic design. She believes the future of school design will be based on research, multi-discipline collaboration, implementation of ideas at multiple scales, and critical evaluation of the impact of learning environments on the users.

Made in the USA
Monee, IL
23 March 2021